Workbook / Laboratory Manual

to accompany

Insieme

Name ______________________________

Exercise 2-1A

Item	Account	Classification
Money in bank	Cash	________
Office supplies	Supplies	________
Money owed	Accounts Payable	________
Office chairs	Office Furniture	________
Net worth of owner	John Smith, Capital	________
Money withdrawn by owner	John Smith, Drawing	________
Money owed by customers	Accounts Receivable	________

Exercise 2-2A

Assets	=	Liabilities	+	Owner's Equity
________	=	$27,000	+	$17,000
$32,000	=	$18,000	+	________
$27,000	=	________	+	$20,000

Exercise 2-3A

	Assets	=	Liabilities	+	Owner's Equity
(a)	________		________		________
Bal.	________		________		________
(b)	________		________		________
Bal.	________		________		________
(c)	________		________		________
	________		________		________
Bal.	________		________		________
(d)	________		________		________
Bal.	________		________		________

Exercise 2-4A

					Owner's Equity							
	Assets	=	Liabilities	+	Capital	–	Drawing	+	Revenues	–	Expenses	Description
Bal. from E 2-3A												
(d)												
(e)												
(f)												
(g)												
(h)												
(i)												
(j)												
(k)												
Bal.												

Name ______________________________

Exercise 2-5A

Account	Classification	Financial Statement
Cash		
Rent Expense		
Accounts Payable		
Service Fees		
Supplies		
Wages Expense		
Ramon Martinez, Drawing		
Ramon Martinez, Capital		
Prepaid Insurance		
Accounts Receivable		

Exercise 2-6A

Exercise 2-7A

Problem 2-8A

	Assets	=	Liabilities	+	Owner's Equity
1.					
2.					
3.					

Problem 2-9A: See page WP-7

Problem 2-10A

Problem 2-9A

	Assets							=	Liabilities	+	Owner's Equity								
	(Items Owned)								(Amts. Owed)		(Owner's Investment)				(Earnings)				
	Cash	+	Accounts Receivable	+	Office Supplies	+	Prepaid Insurance	=	Accounts Payable	+	J. Pembroke, Capital	–	J. Pembroke, Drawing	+	Revenues	–	Expenses		Description
(a)																			
(b)																			
(c)																			
(d)																			
(e)																			
(f)																			
(g)																			
Bal.																			

Problem 2-11A

Problem 2-12A

Name ____________________

Exercise 2-1B

Account	Classification
Cash	____________
Accounts Payable	____________
Supplies	____________
Bill Jones, Drawing	____________
Prepaid Insurance	____________
Accounts Receivable	____________
Bill Jones, Capital	____________

Exercise 2-2B

Assets	=	Liabilities	+	Owner's Equity
____________	=	$20,000	+	$ 5,000
$30,000	=	$15,000	+	____________
$20,000	=	____________	+	$10,000

Exercise 2-3B

	Assets	=	Liabilities	+	Owner's Equity
(a)	____________		____________		____________
Bal.	____________		____________		____________
(b)	____________		____________		____________
Bal.	____________		____________		____________
(c)	____________		____________		____________
	____________		____________		____________
Bal.	____________		____________		____________
(d)	____________		____________		____________
Bal.	____________		____________		____________

Exercise 2-4B

	Assets	=	Liabilities	+	Owner's Equity: Capital	–	Drawing	+	Revenues	–	Expenses	Description
Bal. from E 2-3B												
(d)												
(e)												
(f)												
(g)												
(h)												
(i)												
(j)												
(k)												
Bal.												

Name ______________________________

Exercise 2-5B

Account	Classification	Financial Statement
Cash		
Rent Expense		
Accounts Payable		
Service Fees		
Supplies		
Wages Expense		
Amanda Wong, Drawing		
Amanda Wong, Capital		
Prepaid Insurance		
Accounts Receivable		

Exercise 2-6B

Exercise 2-7B

Problem 2-8B

	Assets	=	Liabilities	+	Owner's Equity
1.					
2.					
3.					

Problem 2-9B: See page WP-13

Problem 2-10B

Problem 2-9B

	Assets				= Liabilities	+	Owner's Equity			
	(Items Owned)				(Amts. Owed)	(Owner's Investment)		(Earnings)		
	Cash	+ Accounts Receivable	+ Office Supplies	+ Prepaid Insurance	= Accounts Payable	+ D. Segal, Capital	– D. Segal, Drawing	+ Revenues	– Expenses	Description
(a)										
(b)										
(c)										
(d)										
(e)										
(f)										
(g)										
Bal.										

Problem 2-11B

Problem 2-12B

Mastery Problem

1.

	Assets						= Liabilities +	Owner's Equity				
	(Items Owned)						(Amts. Owed)	(Owner's Investment)		(Earnings)		
	Cash	+ Accts. Rec.	+ Sup-plies	+ Prepaid Ins.	+ Tools	+ Van	= Accts. Payable	+ L. Vozniak, Capital	− L. Vozniak, Drawing	+ Rev.	− Exp.	Description
(a)												
(b)												
(c)												
(d)												
(e)												
(f)												
(g)												
(h)												
(i)												
(j)												
(k)												
(l)												
(m)												
(n)												
(o)												
(p)												
2. Bal.												

Mastery Problem (Continued)

3.

4.

Name ____________________________________

Mastery Problem (Concluded)

5.

Challenge Problem

Cash from customers		
Cash paid for wages		
Cash paid for rent		
Cash paid for utilities		
Cash paid for insurance		
Cash paid for supplies		
Cash paid for telephone		
Total cash paid for operating items		
Difference between cash received from customers and		
cash paid for goods and services		

Name ______________________________

Exercise 3-1A

Cash	
500	100
400	200
600	

Exercise 3-2A

a. The cash account is increased with a .... ____________

b. The owner's capital account is increased with a .... ____________

c. The delivery equipment account is increased with a .... ____________

d. The cash account is decreased with a .... ____________

e. The liability account Accounts Payable is increased with a .... ____________

f. The revenue account Delivery Fees is increased with a .... ____________

g. The asset account Accounts Receivable is increased with a .... ____________

h. The rent expense account is increased with a .... ____________

i. The owner's drawing account is increased with a .... ____________

Exercise 3-3A

1. and 2.

Cash	

Richard Gibbs, Capital	

Supplies	

Utilities Expense	

Exercise 3-4A

Account	Debit or Credit
1. Cash	________
2. Wages Expense	________
3. Accounts Payable	________
4. Owner's Drawing	________
5. Supplies	________
6. Owner's Capital	________
7. Equipment	________

Exercises 3-5A and 3-6A: See page WP-21

Exercises 3-5A and 3-6A

Assets = Liabilities + Owner's Equity

Assets Dr.	Assets Cr.	Liabilities Dr.	Liabilities Cr.	Owner's Equity Dr.	Owner's Equity Cr.
+	–	–	+	–	+

Drawing Dr.	Drawing Cr.	Expenses Dr.	Expenses Cr.	Revenues Dr.	Revenues Cr.
+	–	+	–	–	+

Exercise 3-7A

Assets		=	Liabilities		+	Owner's Equity	
Dr. +	Cr. –		Dr. –	Cr. +		Dr. –	Cr. +

Drawing		Expenses		Revenues	
Dr. +	Cr. –	Dr. +	Cr. –	Dr. –	Cr. +

Exercise 3-8A

ACCOUNT	DEBIT BALANCE	CREDIT BALANCE

Exercise 3-9A

ACCOUNT	DEBIT BALANCE	CREDIT BALANCE

Exercise 3-10A

Exercise 3-11A

Exercise 3-12A

Problem 3-13A

1. and 2.

Assets		=	Liabilities		+	Owner's Equity	
Dr.	Cr.		Dr.	Cr.		Dr.	Cr.
+	–		–	+		–	+

Drawing		Expenses		Revenues	
Dr.	Cr.	Dr.	Cr.	Dr.	Cr.
+	–	+	–	–	+

Problem 3-13A (Concluded)

3.

ACCOUNT	DEBIT BALANCE	CREDIT BALANCE

Problem 3-14A

1.

a. Total revenue for the month .... ____

b. Total expenses for the month .... ____

c. Net income for the month .... ____

2.

a. Wilhelm Kohl's original investment in the business .... ____

+ Net income for the month .... ____

– Owner's drawing .... ____

Increase in capital .... ____

= Ending owner's equity .... ____

b. End-of-month accounting equation:

Assets	=	Liabilities	+	Owner's Equity
____		____		____

Problem 3-15A

1.

Problem 3-15A (Concluded)

2.

3.

Exercise 3-1B

Accounts Payable

300	450
250	350
	150

Exercise 3-2B

a. The asset account Prepaid Insurance is increased with a .... ______________

b. The owner's drawing account is increased with a .... ______________

c. The asset account Accounts Receivable is decreased with a .... ______________

d. The liability account Accounts Payable is decreased with a.............................. ______________

e. The owner's capital account is increased with a .... ______________

f. The revenue account Professional Fees is increased with a............................ ______________

g. The expense account Repair Expense is increased with a .... ______________

h. The asset account Cash is decreased with a.. ______________

i. The asset account Delivery Equipment is decreased with a.............................. ______________

Exercise 3-3B

1. and 2.

Cash

Roberto Alvarez, Capital

Supplies

Utilities Expense

Name ______________________________

Exercise 3-4B

Account	**Debit or Credit**
1. Cash	____________
2. Rent Expense	____________
3. Notes Payable	____________
4. Owner's Drawing	____________
5. Accounts Receivable	____________
6. Owner's Capital	____________
7. Tools	____________

Exercises 3-5B and 3-6B: See page WP-32

Exercises 3-5B and 3-6B

Assets		=	Liabilities		+	Owner's Equity	
Dr. +	Cr. –		Dr. –	Cr. +		Dr. –	Cr. +

Drawing		Expenses		Revenues	
Dr. +	Cr. –	Dr. +	Cr. –	Dr. –	Cr. +

Exercise 3-7B

Assets		=	Liabilities		+	Owner's Equity	
Dr. +	Cr. –		Dr. –	Cr. +		Dr. –	Cr. +

Drawing		Expenses		Revenues	
Dr. +	Cr. –	Dr. +	Cr. –	Dr. –	Cr. +

Exercise 3-8B

ACCOUNT	DEBIT BALANCE	CREDIT BALANCE

Name ______________________________

Exercise 3-9B

ACCOUNT	DEBIT BALANCE	CREDIT BALANCE

Exercise 3-10B

Exercise 3-11B

Exercise 3-12B

Problem 3-13B
1. and 2.

Assets		=	Liabilities		+	Owner's Equity	
Dr. +	Cr. –		Dr. –	Cr. +		Dr. –	Cr. +

Drawing		Expenses		Revenues	
Dr. +	Cr. –	Dr. +	Cr. –	Dr. –	Cr. +

Problem 3-13B (Concluded)

3.

ACCOUNT	DEBIT BALANCE	CREDIT BALANCE

Problem 3-14B

1.

a. Total revenue for the month .... ____________

b. Total expenses for the month .... ____________

c. Net income for the month .... ____________

2.

a. Sue Jantz's original investment in the business .... ____________

+ Net income for the month .... ____________

– Owner's drawing .... ____________

Increase in capital .... ____________

= Ending owner's equity .... ____________

b. End-of-month accounting equation:

Assets	=	Liabilities	+	Owner's Equity
____________		____________		____________

Problem 3-15B

1.

Problem 3-15B (Concluded)

2.

3.

Mastery Problem

1. and 2.

Assets		=	Liabilities		+	Owner's Equity	
Dr. +	Cr. –		Dr. –	Cr. +		Dr. –	Cr. +

Drawing		Expenses		Revenues	
Dr. +	Cr. –	Dr. +	Cr. –	Dr. –	Cr. +

Mastery Problem (Continued)

3.

ACCOUNT	DEBIT BALANCE	CREDIT BALANCE

4.

Name ______________________________

Mastery Problem (Concluded)

5.

6.

Challenge Problem

1.

2.

Exercise 4-1A

1.	____________	Check stubs or check register	a. A good or service has been sold.
2.	____________	Purchase invoice from suppliers (vendors)	b. Cash has been received by the business.
3.	____________	Sales tickets or invoices to customers	c. Cash has been paid by the business.
4.	____________	Receipts or cash register tapes	d. Goods or services have been purchased by the business.

Exercise 4-2A

Transaction	Debit	Credit
1. Invested cash in the business, $5,000.	____________	____________
2. Paid office rent, $500.	____________	____________
3. Purchased office supplies on account, $300.	____________	____________
4. Received cash for services rendered (fees), $400.	____________	____________
5. Paid cash on account, $50.	____________	____________
6. Rendered services on account, $300.	____________	____________
7. Received cash for an amount owed by a customer, $100.	____________	____________

Exercise 4-3A

Exercise 4-3A (Concluded)

Total Debits: **Total Credits:**

Exercise 4-4A

GENERAL JOURNAL

PAGE 1

	DATE		DESCRIPTION	POST. REF.	DEBIT	CREDIT	
1							1
2							2
3							3
4							4
5							5
6							6
7							7
8							8
9							9
10							10
11							11
12							12
13							13
14							14
15							15
16							16
17							17
18							18
19							19
20							20
21							21
22							22
23							23
24							24

Name ______________________

Exercise 4-4A (Concluded)

GENERAL JOURNAL

PAGE 2

	DATE	DESCRIPTION	POST. REF.	DEBIT	CREDIT	
1						1
2						2
3						3
4						4
5						5
6						6
7						7
8						8
9						9
10						10
11						11
12						12
13						13
14						14
15						15
16						16
17						17
18						18
19						19
20						20
21						21
22						22
23						23
24						24
25						25
26						26
27						27
28						28
29						29
30						30
31						31
32						32
33						33
34						34
35						35
36						36

Exercise 4-5A

GENERAL LEDGER

ACCOUNT ACCOUNT NO.

DATE	ITEM	POST. REF.	DEBIT	CREDIT	BALANCE DEBIT	BALANCE CREDIT

ACCOUNT ACCOUNT NO.

DATE	ITEM	POST. REF.	DEBIT	CREDIT	BALANCE DEBIT	BALANCE CREDIT

ACCOUNT ACCOUNT NO.

DATE	ITEM	POST. REF.	DEBIT	CREDIT	BALANCE DEBIT	BALANCE CREDIT

Name ______________________________

Exercise 4-5A (Continued)

ACCOUNT ______________________________ ACCOUNT NO. ________

DATE		ITEM	POST. REF.	DEBIT	CREDIT	BALANCE	
						DEBIT	CREDIT

ACCOUNT ______________________________ ACCOUNT NO. ________

DATE		ITEM	POST. REF.	DEBIT	CREDIT	BALANCE	
						DEBIT	CREDIT

ACCOUNT ______________________________ ACCOUNT NO. ________

DATE		ITEM	POST. REF.	DEBIT	CREDIT	BALANCE	
						DEBIT	CREDIT

ACCOUNT ______________________________ ACCOUNT NO. ________

DATE		ITEM	POST. REF.	DEBIT	CREDIT	BALANCE	
						DEBIT	CREDIT

Exercise 4-5A (Continued)

ACCOUNT ACCOUNT NO.

DATE		ITEM	POST. REF.	DEBIT	CREDIT	BALANCE DEBIT	BALANCE CREDIT

ACCOUNT ACCOUNT NO.

DATE		ITEM	POST. REF.	DEBIT	CREDIT	BALANCE DEBIT	BALANCE CREDIT

ACCOUNT ACCOUNT NO.

DATE		ITEM	POST. REF.	DEBIT	CREDIT	BALANCE DEBIT	BALANCE CREDIT

ACCOUNT ACCOUNT NO.

DATE		ITEM	POST. REF.	DEBIT	CREDIT	BALANCE DEBIT	BALANCE CREDIT

ACCOUNT ACCOUNT NO.

DATE		ITEM	POST. REF.	DEBIT	CREDIT	BALANCE DEBIT	BALANCE CREDIT

Name ____________________

Exercise 4-5A (Concluded)

ACCOUNT TITLE	ACCT. NO.	DEBIT BALANCE	CREDIT BALANCE

Exercise 4-6A

Exercise 4-6A (Concluded)

Name ______________________________

Exercise 4-7A

Exercise 4-7A (Concluded)

Exercise 4-8A

GENERAL JOURNAL

PAGE

DATE		DESCRIPTION	POST. REF.	DEBIT	CREDIT
May	17	Office Equipment		400 00	
		Cash			400 00
		Purchased copy paper			
	23	Cash	101	1000 00	
		Service Fees	401		1000 00
		Received cash for services previously earned			

Problem 4-9A

2. **(For 1. and 3., see page WP-58.)**

GENERAL JOURNAL

PAGE 1

DATE		DESCRIPTION	POST. REF.	DEBIT	CREDIT

Problem 4-9A (Continued)

GENERAL JOURNAL

PAGE 2

DATE		DESCRIPTION	POST. REF.	DEBIT	CREDIT

Problem 4-9A (Continued)

GENERAL JOURNAL

PAGE 3

DATE		DESCRIPTION	POST. REF.	DEBIT	CREDIT

Problm 4-9A (Continued)

1. and 3.

GENERAL LEDGER

ACCOUNT Cash ACCOUNT NO. 101

DATE	ITEM	POST. REF.	DEBIT	CREDIT	BALANCE DEBIT	BALANCE CREDIT

ACCOUNT Office Supplies ACCOUNT NO. 142

DATE	ITEM	POST. REF.	DEBIT	CREDIT	BALANCE DEBIT	BALANCE CREDIT

Problem 4-9A (Continued)

ACCOUNT Office Equipment ACCOUNT NO. 181

DATE		ITEM	POST. REF.	DEBIT	CREDIT	BALANCE DEBIT	BALANCE CREDIT

ACCOUNT Accounts Payable ACCOUNT NO. 202

DATE		ITEM	POST. REF.	DEBIT	CREDIT	BALANCE DEBIT	BALANCE CREDIT

ACCOUNT Annette Creighton, Capital ACCOUNT NO. 311

DATE		ITEM	POST. REF.	DEBIT	CREDIT	BALANCE DEBIT	BALANCE CREDIT

ACCOUNT Annette Creighton, Drawing ACCOUNT NO. 312

DATE		ITEM	POST. REF.	DEBIT	CREDIT	BALANCE DEBIT	BALANCE CREDIT

Problem 4-9A (Continued)

ACCOUNT Consulting Fees ACCOUNT NO. 401

DATE		ITEM	POST. REF.	DEBIT	CREDIT	BALANCE DEBIT	BALANCE CREDIT

ACCOUNT Wages Expense ACCOUNT NO. 511

DATE		ITEM	POST. REF.	DEBIT	CREDIT	BALANCE DEBIT	BALANCE CREDIT

ACCOUNT Advertising Expense ACCOUNT NO. 512

DATE		ITEM	POST. REF.	DEBIT	CREDIT	BALANCE DEBIT	BALANCE CREDIT

ACCOUNT Rent Expense ACCOUNT NO. 521

DATE		ITEM	POST. REF.	DEBIT	CREDIT	BALANCE DEBIT	BALANCE CREDIT

Problem 4-9A (Continued)

ACCOUNT Telephone Expense ACCOUNT NO. 525

DATE	ITEM	POST. REF.	DEBIT	CREDIT	BALANCE DEBIT	BALANCE CREDIT

ACCOUNT Transportation Expense ACCOUNT NO 526

DATE	ITEM	POST. REF.	DEBIT	CREDIT	BALANCE DEBIT	BALANCE CREDIT

ACCOUNT Utilities Expense ACCOUNT NO. 533

DATE	ITEM	POST. REF.	DEBIT	CREDIT	BALANCE DEBIT	BALANCE CREDIT

ACCOUNT Miscellaneous Expense ACCOUNT NO. 549

DATE	ITEM	POST. REF.	DEBIT	CREDIT	BALANCE DEBIT	BALANCE CREDIT

Problem 4-9A (Continued)

4.

ACCOUNT TITLE	ACCT. NO.	DEBIT BALANCE	CREDIT BALANCE

Problem 4-9A (Continued)

5.

Problem 4-9A (Concluded)

Name ______________________________

Problem 4-10A

2. (For 1. and 3., see page WP-68.)

GENERAL JOURNAL

PAGE 7

	DATE		DESCRIPTION	POST. REF.	DEBIT	CREDIT	
1							1
2							2
3							3
4							4
5							5
6							6
7							7
8							8
9							9
10							10
11							11
12							12
13							13
14							14
15							15
16							16
17							17
18							18
19							19
20							20
21							21
22							22
23							23
24							24
25							25
26							26
27							27
28							28
29							29
30							30
31							31
32							32
33							33
34							34

Problem 4-10A (Continued)

GENERAL JOURNAL

PAGE 8

DATE		DESCRIPTION	POST. REF.	DEBIT	CREDIT

Problem 4-10A (Continued)

GENERAL JOURNAL

PAGE 9

	DATE		DESCRIPTION	POST. REF.	DEBIT	CREDIT	
1							1
2							2
3							3
4							4
5							5
6							6
7							7
8							8
9							9
10							10
11							11
12							12
13							13
14							14
15							15
16							16
17							17
18							18
19							19
20							20
21							21
22							22
23							23
24							24
25							25
26							26
27							27
28							28
29							29
30							30
31							31
32							32
33							33
34							34
35							35
36							36

Problem 4-10A (Continued)

1. and 3.

ACCOUNT Cash **GENERAL LEDGER** ACCOUNT NO. 101

DATE	ITEM	POST. REF.	DEBIT	CREDIT	BALANCE DEBIT	BALANCE CREDIT

Problem 4-10A (Continued)

ACCOUNT Accounts Receivable ACCOUNT NO. 122

DATE	ITEM	POST. REF.	DEBIT	CREDIT	BALANCE DEBIT	BALANCE CREDIT

ACCOUNT Office Supplies ACCOUNT NO. 142

DATE	ITEM	POST. REF.	DEBIT	CREDIT	BALANCE DEBIT	BALANCE CREDIT

ACCOUNT Office Equipment ACCOUNT NO. 181

DATE	ITEM	POST. REF.	DEBIT	CREDIT	BALANCE DEBIT	BALANCE CREDIT

ACCOUNT Delivery Truck ACCOUNT NO. 185

DATE	ITEM	POST. REF.	DEBIT	CREDIT	BALANCE DEBIT	BALANCE CREDIT

Problem 4-10A (Continued)

ACCOUNT Accounts Payable ACCOUNT NO. 202

DATE	ITEM	POST. REF.	DEBIT	CREDIT	BALANCE DEBIT	BALANCE CREDIT

ACCOUNT Jim Andrews, Capital ACCOUNT NO. 311

DATE	ITEM	POST. REF.	DEBIT	CREDIT	BALANCE DEBIT	BALANCE CREDIT

ACCOUNT Jim Andrews, Drawing ACCOUNT NO. 312

DATE	ITEM	POST. REF.	DEBIT	CREDIT	BALANCE DEBIT	BALANCE CREDIT

ACCOUNT Delivery Fees ACCOUNT NO. 401

DATE	ITEM	POST. REF.	DEBIT	CREDIT	BALANCE DEBIT	BALANCE CREDIT

Name ______________________________

Problem 4-10A (Continued)

ACCOUNT Wages Expense ACCOUNT NO. 511

DATE		ITEM	POST. REF.	DEBIT	CREDIT	BALANCE DEBIT	BALANCE CREDIT

ACCOUNT Advertising Expense ACCOUNT NO. 512

DATE		ITEM	POST. REF.	DEBIT	CREDIT	BALANCE DEBIT	BALANCE CREDIT

ACCOUNT Rent Expense ACCOUNT NO. 521

DATE		ITEM	POST. REF.	DEBIT	CREDIT	BALANCE DEBIT	BALANCE CREDIT

ACCOUNT Telephone Expense ACCOUNT NO. 525

DATE		ITEM	POST. REF.	DEBIT	CREDIT	BALANCE DEBIT	BALANCE CREDIT

Problem 4-10A (Continued)

ACCOUNT Electricity Expense ACCOUNT NO. 533

DATE		ITEM	POST. REF.	DEBIT	CREDIT	BALANCE DEBIT	BALANCE CREDIT

ACCOUNT Charitable Contributions Expense ACCOUNT NO. 534

DATE		ITEM	POST. REF.	DEBIT	CREDIT	BALANCE DEBIT	BALANCE CREDIT

ACCOUNT Gas and Oil Expense ACCOUNT NO. 538

DATE		ITEM	POST. REF.	DEBIT	CREDIT	BALANCE DEBIT	BALANCE CREDIT

ACCOUNT Miscellaneous Expense ACCOUNT NO. 549

DATE		ITEM	POST. REF.	DEBIT	CREDIT	BALANCE DEBIT	BALANCE CREDIT

Problem 4-10A (Concluded)

4.

ACCOUNT TITLE	ACCT. NO.	DEBIT BALANCE	CREDIT BALANCE

Problem 4-11A

GENERAL JOURNAL PAGE

	DATE		DESCRIPTION	POST. REF.	DEBIT	CREDIT	
1							1
2							2
3							3
4							4
5							5
6							6
7							7
8							8
9							9
10							10
11							11
12							12
13							13
14							14
15							15
16							16
17							17
18							18
19							19
20							20

Exercise 4-1B

1. Cash register tape

2. Sales ticket (issued to customer)

3. Purchase invoice (received from supplier or vendor)

4. Check stub

Name ______________________

Exercise 4-2B

Transaction	Debit	Credit
1. Invested cash in the business, $1,000.		
2. Performed services on account, $200.		
3. Purchased office equipment on account, $500.		
4. Received cash on account for services previously rendered, $200.		
5. Made a payment on account, $100.		

Exercise 4-3B

Total Debits:	Total Credits:

Exercise 4-4B

GENERAL JOURNAL

PAGE 1

DATE		DESCRIPTION	POST. REF.	DEBIT	CREDIT

Name ______________________________

Exercise 4-4B (Concluded)

GENERAL JOURNAL

PAGE 2

	DATE		DESCRIPTION	POST. REF.	DEBIT	CREDIT	
1							1
2							2
3							3
4							4
5							5
6							6
7							7
8							8
9							9
10							10
11							11
12							12
13							13
14							14
15							15
16							16
17							17
18							18
19							19
20							20
21							21
22							22
23							23
24							24
25							25
26							26
27							27
28							28
29							29
30							30
31							31
32							32
33							33
34							34
35							35
36							36

Exercise 4-5B

GENERAL LEDGER

ACCOUNT ACCOUNT NO.

DATE		ITEM	POST. REF.	DEBIT	CREDIT	BALANCE DEBIT	BALANCE CREDIT

ACCOUNT ACCOUNT NO.

DATE		ITEM	POST. REF.	DEBIT	CREDIT	BALANCE DEBIT	BALANCE CREDIT

ACCOUNT ACCOUNT NO.

DATE		ITEM	POST. REF.	DEBIT	CREDIT	BALANCE DEBIT	BALANCE CREDIT

Name ______________________________

Exercise 4-5B (Continued)

ACCOUNT ______________________________ ACCOUNT NO. ______

DATE	ITEM	POST. REF.	DEBIT	CREDIT	BALANCE DEBIT	BALANCE CREDIT

ACCOUNT ______________________________ ACCOUNT NO. ______

DATE	ITEM	POST. REF.	DEBIT	CREDIT	BALANCE DEBIT	BALANCE CREDIT

ACCOUNT ______________________________ ACCOUNT NO. ______

DATE	ITEM	POST. REF.	DEBIT	CREDIT	BALANCE DEBIT	BALANCE CREDIT

ACCOUNT ______________________________ ACCOUNT NO. ______

DATE	ITEM	POST. REF.	DEBIT	CREDIT	BALANCE DEBIT	BALANCE CREDIT

Exercise 4-5B (Continued)

ACCOUNT | ACCOUNT NO.

DATE		ITEM	POST. REF.	DEBIT	CREDIT	BALANCE DEBIT	BALANCE CREDIT

ACCOUNT | ACCOUNT NO.

DATE		ITEM	POST. REF.	DEBIT	CREDIT	BALANCE DEBIT	BALANCE CREDIT

ACCOUNT | ACCOUNT NO.

DATE		ITEM	POST. REF.	DEBIT	CREDIT	BALANCE DEBIT	BALANCE CREDIT

ACCOUNT | ACCOUNT NO.

DATE		ITEM	POST. REF.	DEBIT	CREDIT	BALANCE DEBIT	BALANCE CREDIT

ACCOUNT | ACCOUNT NO.

DATE		ITEM	POST. REF.	DEBIT	CREDIT	BALANCE DEBIT	BALANCE CREDIT

Name ______________________________

Exercise 4-5B (Concluded)

ACCOUNT TITLE	ACCT. NO.	DEBIT BALANCE	CREDIT BALANCE

Exercise 4-6B

Exercise 4-6B (Concluded)

Name ______________________________

Exercise 4-7B

Exercise 4-7B (Concluded)

Exercise 4-8B

GENERAL JOURNAL PAGE

DATE		DESCRIPTION	POST. REF.	DEBIT	CREDIT
Apr.	6	Office Supplies		530 00	
		Cash			530 00
		Purchased office equipment			
	21	Cash	101	300 00	
		Service Fees	401		300 00
		Revenue earned from services			
		previously rendered			

Problem 4-9B

2. (For 1. and 3., see page WP-88.)

GENERAL JOURNAL

PAGE 1

	DATE		DESCRIPTION	POST. REF.	DEBIT	CREDIT	
1							1
2							2
3							3
4							4
5							5
6							6
7							7
8							8
9							9
10							10
11							11
12							12
13							13
14							14
15							15
16							16
17							17
18							18
19							19
20							20
21							21
22							22
23							23
24							24
25							25
26							26
27							27
28							28
29							29
30							30
31							31
32							32
33							33
34							34
35							35
36							36

Problem 4-9B (Continued)

GENERAL JOURNAL

PAGE 2

DATE		DESCRIPTION	POST. REF.	DEBIT	CREDIT

Problem 4-9B (Continued)

GENERAL JOURNAL

PAGE 3

DATE		DESCRIPTION	POST. REF.	DEBIT	CREDIT

Problem 4-9B (Continued)

1. and 3.

GENERAL LEDGER

ACCOUNT Cash ACCOUNT NO. 101

DATE	ITEM	POST. REF.	DEBIT	CREDIT	BALANCE DEBIT	BALANCE CREDIT

ACCOUNT Accounts Receivable ACCOUNT NO. 122

DATE	ITEM	POST. REF.	DEBIT	CREDIT	BALANCE DEBIT	BALANCE CREDIT

Name ______________________________

Problem 4-9B (Continued)

ACCOUNT Office Supplies ACCOUNT NO. 142

DATE		ITEM	POST. REF.	DEBIT	CREDIT	BALANCE DEBIT	BALANCE CREDIT

ACCOUNT Office Equipment ACCOUNT NO. 181

DATE		ITEM	POST. REF.	DEBIT	CREDIT	BALANCE DEBIT	BALANCE CREDIT

ACCOUNT Accounts Payable ACCOUNT NO. 202

DATE		ITEM	POST. REF.	DEBIT	CREDIT	BALANCE DEBIT	BALANCE CREDIT

ACCOUNT Benito Mendez, Capital ACCOUNT NO. 311

DATE		ITEM	POST. REF.	DEBIT	CREDIT	BALANCE DEBIT	BALANCE CREDIT

Problem 4-9B (Continued)

ACCOUNT Benito Mendez, Drawing ACCOUNT NO. 312

DATE		ITEM	POST. REF.	DEBIT	CREDIT	BALANCE DEBIT	BALANCE CREDIT

ACCOUNT Appraisal Fees ACCOUNT NO. 401

DATE		ITEM	POST. REF.	DEBIT	CREDIT	BALANCE DEBIT	BALANCE CREDIT

ACCOUNT Wages Expense ACCOUNT NO. 511

DATE		ITEM	POST. REF.	DEBIT	CREDIT	BALANCE DEBIT	BALANCE CREDIT

ACCOUNT Advertising Expense ACCOUNT NO. 512

DATE		ITEM	POST. REF.	DEBIT	CREDIT	BALANCE DEBIT	BALANCE CREDIT

Problem 4-9B (Continued)

ACCOUNT Rent Expense ACCOUNT NO. 521

DATE	ITEM	POST. REF.	DEBIT	CREDIT	BALANCE DEBIT	BALANCE CREDIT

ACCOUNT Telephone Expense ACCOUNT NO. 525

DATE	ITEM	POST. REF.	DEBIT	CREDIT	BALANCE DEBIT	BALANCE CREDIT

ACCOUNT Transportation Expense ACCOUNT NO 526

DATE	ITEM	POST. REF.	DEBIT	CREDIT	BALANCE DEBIT	BALANCE CREDIT

ACCOUNT Electricity Expense ACCOUNT NO. 533

DATE	ITEM	POST. REF.	DEBIT	CREDIT	BALANCE DEBIT	BALANCE CREDIT

ACCOUNT Miscellaneous Expense ACCOUNT NO. 549

DATE	ITEM	POST. REF.	DEBIT	CREDIT	BALANCE DEBIT	BALANCE CREDIT

Problem 4-9B (Continued)

4.

ACCOUNT TITLE	ACCT. NO.	DEBIT BALANCE	CREDIT BALANCE

Problem 4-9B (Continued)

5.

Problem 4-9B (Concluded)

Problem 4-10B

2. **(For 1. and 3., see page WP-98.)**

GENERAL JOURNAL

PAGE 7

DATE		DESCRIPTION	POST. REF.	DEBIT	CREDIT

Problem 4-10B (Continued)

GENERAL JOURNAL

PAGE 8

DATE		DESCRIPTION	POST. REF.	DEBIT	CREDIT

Problem 4-10B (Continued)

GENERAL JOURNAL

PAGE 9

	DATE		DESCRIPTION	POST. REF.	DEBIT	CREDIT	
1							1
2							2
3							3
4							4
5							5
6							6
7							7
8							8
9							9
10							10
11							11
12							12
13							13
14							14
15							15
16							16
17							17
18							18
19							19
20							20
21							21
22							22
23							23
24							24
25							25
26							26
27							27
28							28
29							29
30							30
31							31
32							32
33							33
34							34
35							35
36							36

Problem 4-10B (Continued)

1. and 3.

GENERAL LEDGER

ACCOUNT Cash ACCOUNT NO. 101

DATE		ITEM	POST. REF.	DEBIT	CREDIT	BALANCE DEBIT	BALANCE CREDIT

ACCOUNT Accounts Receivable ACCOUNT NO. 122

DATE		ITEM	POST. REF.	DEBIT	CREDIT	BALANCE DEBIT	BALANCE CREDIT

Problem 4-10B (Continued)

ACCOUNT Tailoring Supplies ACCOUNT NO. 141

DATE	ITEM	POST. REF.	DEBIT	CREDIT	BALANCE DEBIT	BALANCE CREDIT

ACCOUNT Tailoring Equipment ACCOUNT NO. 183

DATE	ITEM	POST. REF.	DEBIT	CREDIT	BALANCE DEBIT	BALANCE CREDIT

ACCOUNT Accounts Payable ACCOUNT NO. 202

DATE	ITEM	POST. REF.	DEBIT	CREDIT	BALANCE DEBIT	BALANCE CREDIT

ACCOUNT Ann Taylor, Capital ACCOUNT NO. 311

DATE	ITEM	POST. REF.	DEBIT	CREDIT	BALANCE DEBIT	BALANCE CREDIT

Problem 4-10B (Continued)

ACCOUNT Ann Taylor, Drawing — ACCOUNT NO. 312

DATE	ITEM	POST. REF.	DEBIT	CREDIT	BALANCE DEBIT	BALANCE CREDIT

ACCOUNT Tailoring Fees — ACCOUNT NO. 401

DATE	ITEM	POST. REF.	DEBIT	CREDIT	BALANCE DEBIT	BALANCE CREDIT

ACCOUNT Wages Expense — ACCOUNT NO. 511

DATE	ITEM	POST. REF.	DEBIT	CREDIT	BALANCE DEBIT	BALANCE CREDIT

ACCOUNT Advertising Expense — ACCOUNT NO. 512

DATE	ITEM	POST. REF.	DEBIT	CREDIT	BALANCE DEBIT	BALANCE CREDIT

Name ______________________________

Problem 4-10B (Continued)

ACCOUNT Rent Expense ACCOUNT NO. 521

DATE		ITEM	POST. REF.	DEBIT	CREDIT	BALANCE DEBIT	BALANCE CREDIT

ACCOUNT Telephone Expense ACCOUNT NO. 525

DATE		ITEM	POST. REF.	DEBIT	CREDIT	BALANCE DEBIT	BALANCE CREDIT

ACCOUNT Electricity Expense ACCOUNT NO. 533

DATE		ITEM	POST. REF.	DEBIT	CREDIT	BALANCE DEBIT	BALANCE CREDIT

ACCOUNT Miscellaneous Expense ACCOUNT NO. 549

DATE		ITEM	POST. REF.	DEBIT	CREDIT	BALANCE DEBIT	BALANCE CREDIT

Problem 4-10B (Concluded)

4.

ACCOUNT TITLE	ACCT. NO.	DEBIT BALANCE	CREDIT BALANCE

Problem 4-11B

GENERAL JOURNAL

PAGE

	DATE		DESCRIPTION	POST. REF.	DEBIT	CREDIT	
1							1
2							2
3							3
4							4
5							5
6							6
7							7
8							8
9							9
10							10
11							11
12							12
13							13
14							14
15							15
16							16
17							17
18							18
19							19
20							20
21							21
22							22
23							23

Mastery Problem

1.

GENERAL JOURNAL

PAGE 1

DATE		DESCRIPTION	POST. REF.	DEBIT	CREDIT

Name ______________________________

Mastery Problem (Continued)

GENERAL JOURNAL

PAGE 2

	DATE		DESCRIPTION	POST. REF.	DEBIT	CREDIT	
1							1
2							2
3							3
4							4
5							5
6							6
7							7
8							8
9							9
10							10
11							11
12							12
13							13
14							14
15							15
16							16
17							17
18							18
19							19
20							20
21							21
22							22
23							23
24							24
25							25
26							26
27							27
28							28
29							29
30							30
31							31
32							32
33							33
34							34
35							35

Mastery Problem (Continued)

GENERAL JOURNAL

PAGE 3

	DATE		DESCRIPTION	POST. REF.	DEBIT	CREDIT	
1							1
2							2
3							3
4							4
5							5
6							6
7							7
8							8
9							9
10							10
11							11
12							12
13							13
14							14
15							15
16							16
17							17
18							18
19							19
20							20
21							21
22							22
23							23
24							24
25							25
26							26
27							27
28							28
29							29
30							30
31							31
32							32
33							33
34							34
35							35

Mastery Problem (Continued)

2.

ACCOUNT Cash **GENERAL LEDGER** ACCOUNT NO. 101

DATE	ITEM	POST. REF.	DEBIT	CREDIT	BALANCE	
					DEBIT	CREDIT

ACCOUNT Office Supplies ACCOUNT NO. 142

DATE	ITEM	POST. REF.	DEBIT	CREDIT	BALANCE	
					DEBIT	CREDIT

ACCOUNT Athletic Equipment ACCOUNT NO. 183

DATE	ITEM	POST. REF.	DEBIT	CREDIT	BALANCE	
					DEBIT	CREDIT

Mastery Problem (Continued)

ACCOUNT Basketball Facilities ACCOUNT NO. 184

DATE		ITEM	POST. REF.	DEBIT	CREDIT	BALANCE DEBIT	BALANCE CREDIT

ACCOUNT Accounts Payable ACCOUNT NO. 202

DATE		ITEM	POST. REF.	DEBIT	CREDIT	BALANCE DEBIT	BALANCE CREDIT

ACCOUNT Barry Bird, Capital ACCOUNT NO. 311

DATE		ITEM	POST. REF.	DEBIT	CREDIT	BALANCE DEBIT	BALANCE CREDIT

ACCOUNT Barry Bird, Drawing ACCOUNT NO. 312

DATE		ITEM	POST. REF.	DEBIT	CREDIT	BALANCE DEBIT	BALANCE CREDIT

Mastery Problem (Continued)

ACCOUNT Registration Fees ACCOUNT NO. 401

DATE		ITEM	POST. REF.	DEBIT	CREDIT	BALANCE	
						DEBIT	CREDIT

ACCOUNT Wages Expense ACCOUNT NO. 511

DATE		ITEM	POST. REF.	DEBIT	CREDIT	BALANCE	
						DEBIT	CREDIT

ACCOUNT Advertising Expense ACCOUNT NO. 512

DATE		ITEM	POST. REF.	DEBIT	CREDIT	BALANCE	
						DEBIT	CREDIT

Mastery Problem (Continued)

ACCOUNT Food Expense ACCOUNT NO. 524

DATE		ITEM	POST. REF.	DEBIT	CREDIT	BALANCE DEBIT	BALANCE CREDIT

ACCOUNT Telephone Expense ACCOUNT NO. 525

DATE		ITEM	POST. REF.	DEBIT	CREDIT	BALANCE DEBIT	BALANCE CREDIT

ACCOUNT Utilities Expense ACCOUNT NO. 533

DATE		ITEM	POST. REF.	DEBIT	CREDIT	BALANCE DEBIT	BALANCE CREDIT

ACCOUNT Postage Expense ACCOUNT NO. 536

DATE		ITEM	POST. REF.	DEBIT	CREDIT	BALANCE DEBIT	BALANCE CREDIT

Name ______________________________

Mastery Problem (Concluded)

3.

ACCOUNT TITLE	ACCT. NO.	DEBIT BALANCE	CREDIT BALANCE

Challenge Problem

1. and 2.

3.

Fred Phaler Consulting

Trial Balance

June 30, 20--

ACCOUNT TITLE	ACCT. NO.	DEBIT BALANCE	CREDIT BALANCE
Cash	101		
Accounts Receivable	122		
Office Supplies	142		
Accounts Payable	202		
Fred Phaler, Capital	311		
Fred Phaler, Drawing	312		
Professional Fees	401		
Wages Expense	511		
Rent Expense	521		
Telephone Expense	525		
Automobile Expense	526		
Utilities Expense	533		

Name ______________________________

Exercise 5-1A

(Balance Sheet) Supplies	(Income Statement) Supplies Expense

GENERAL JOURNAL

PAGE

	DATE		DESCRIPTION	POST. REF.	DEBIT	CREDIT	
1							1
2							2
3							3
4							4
5							5
6							6

Exercise 5-2A

(Balance Sheet) Prepaid Insurance	(Income Statement) Insurance Expense

GENERAL JOURNAL

PAGE

	DATE		DESCRIPTION	POST. REF.	DEBIT	CREDIT	
1							1
2							2
3							3
4							4
5							5
6							6

Exercise 5-3A

(Income Statement)
Wages Expense

(Balance Sheet)
Wages Payable

GENERAL JOURNAL PAGE

	DATE		DESCRIPTION	POST. REF.	DEBIT	CREDIT	
1							1
2							2
3							3
4							4

Exercise 5-4A

(Income Statement)
Depr. Expense—Delivery Equipment

(Balance Sheet)
Accum. Depr.—Delivery Equipment

GENERAL JOURNAL PAGE

	DATE		DESCRIPTION	POST. REF.	DEBIT	CREDIT	
1							1
2							2
3							3
4							4

Exercise 5-5A

Name ______________________________

Exercise 5-6A

1.

(Balance Sheet) Supplies		
TB	580	
Bal.		

(Income Statement) Supplies Expense	

2.

(Balance Sheet) Supplies		
TB	435	
Bal.		

(Income Statement) Supplies Expense	

Exercise 5-7A

1.

(Balance Sheet) Prepaid Insurance		
TB	1,450	
Bal.		

(Income Statement) Insurance Expense	

2.

(Balance Sheet) Prepaid Insurance		
TB	1,350	
Bal.		

(Income Statement) Insurance Expense	

Exercise 5-8A

GENERAL JOURNAL

PAGE 9

	DATE		DESCRIPTION	POST. REF.	DEBIT	CREDIT	
1			Adjusting Entries				1
2	20-- Dec.	31	Supplies Expense		85 00		2
3			Supplies			85 00	3
4							4
5		31	Wages Expense		220 00		5
6			Wages Payable			220 00	6
7							7
8							8
9							9
10							10
11							11
12							12
13							13
14							14
15							15
16							16
17							17
18							18

Exercise 5-8A (Concluded)

GENERAL LEDGER

ACCOUNT Supplies ACCOUNT NO. 141

DATE		ITEM	POST. REF.	DEBIT	CREDIT	BALANCE DEBIT	BALANCE CREDIT
20-- Dec.	1	Balance	✓			150 00	
	15		J8	50 00		200 00	

ACCOUNT Wages Payable ACCOUNT NO. 219

DATE		ITEM	POST. REF.	DEBIT	CREDIT	BALANCE DEBIT	BALANCE CREDIT

ACCOUNT Wages Expense ACCOUNT NO. 511

DATE		ITEM	POST. REF.	DEBIT	CREDIT	BALANCE DEBIT	BALANCE CREDIT
20-- Dec.	1	Balance	✓			900 00	
	15		J8	300 00		1200 00	

ACCOUNT Supplies Expense ACCOUNT NO. 523

DATE		ITEM	POST. REF.	DEBIT	CREDIT	BALANCE DEBIT	BALANCE CREDIT

Exercise 5-9A

Jim Jacobs' Furniture Repair
Work Sheet (Partial)
For Year Ended December 31, 20--

ACCOUNT TITLE	TRIAL BALANCE		ADJUSTMENTS		ADJUSTED TRIAL BALANCE	
	DEBIT	CREDIT	DEBIT	CREDIT	DEBIT	CREDIT
Cash	100 00				100 00	
Supplies	850 00				200 00	
Prepaid Insurance	900 00				300 00	
Delivery Equipment	3 600 00				3 600 00	
Accum. Depr.—Delivery Equip.		600 00				800 00
Wages Payable						100 00
Jim Jacobs, Capital		4 000 00				4 000 00
Repair Fees		1 650 00				1 650 00
Wages Expense	600 00				700 00	
Advertising Expense	200 00				200 00	
Supplies Expense					650 00	
Insurance Expense					600 00	
Depr. Exp.—Delivery Equip.					200 00	
	6 250 00	6 250 00			6 550 00	6 550 00

Exercise 5-10A

GENERAL JOURNAL

PAGE

	DATE		DESCRIPTION	POST. REF.	DEBIT	CREDIT	
1							1
2							2
3							3
4							4
5							5
6							6
7							7
8							8
9							9
10							10
11							11
12							12
13							13
14							14
15							15

Exercise 5-11A

	Income Statement		Balance Sheet	
	Debit	Credit	Debit	Credit
Cash				
Accounts Receivable				
Supplies				
Prepaid Insurance				
Delivery Equipment				
Accum. Depr.—Delivery Equip.				
Accounts Payable				
Wages Payable				
Owner, Capital				
Owner, Drawing				
Delivery Fees				
Wages Expense				
Rent Expense				
Supplies Expense				
Insurance Expense				
Depr. Exp.—Delivery Equip.				

Exercise 5-12A

	Income Statement		Balance Sheet	
	Debit	Credit	Debit	Credit
Net Income				
Net Loss				

Exercise 5-13A

	Cash Basis	Modified Cash Basis	Accrual Basis
1. Purchase supplies on account.			
2. Make payment on asset previously purchased.			
3. Purchase supplies for cash.			
4. Purchase insurance for cash.			
5. Pay cash for wages.			
6. Pay cash for telephone expense.			
7. Pay cash for new equipment.			
8. Wages earned but not paid.			
9. Prepaid item purchased, partly used.			
10. Depreciation on long-term assets.			

Problem 5-14A

Mason's Delivery

Work

For Month Ended

	ACCOUNT TITLE	TRIAL BALANCE DEBIT	TRIAL BALANCE CREDIT	ADJUSTMENTS DEBIT	ADJUSTMENTS CREDIT
1	Cash	1,600.00			
2	Accounts Receivable	940.00			
3	Supplies	635.00			
4	Prepaid Insurance	1,200.00			
5	Delivery Equipment	6,400.00			
6	Accum. Depr.—Delivery Equip.				
7	Accounts Payable		1,220.00		
8	Wages Payable				
9	Jill Mason, Capital		8,000.00		
10	Jill Mason, Drawing	1,400.00			
11	Delivery Fees		6,200.00		
12	Wages Expense	1,500.00			
13	Advertising Expense	460.00			
14	Rent Expense	800.00			
15	Supplies Expense				
16	Telephone Expense	165.00			
17	Insurance Expense				
18	Repair Expense	230.00			
19	Oil and Gas Expense	90.00			
20	Depr. Exp.—Delivery Equip.				
21		15,420.00	15,420.00		
22					
23					
24					
25					
26					
27					
28					
29					
30					
31					
32					
33					

Problem 5-14A (Concluded)

Service

Sheet

September 30, 20--

ADJUSTED TRIAL BALANCE		INCOME STATEMENT		BALANCE SHEET		
DEBIT	CREDIT	DEBIT	CREDIT	DEBIT	CREDIT	
						1
						2
						3
						4
						5
						6
						7
						8
						9
						10
						11
						12
						13
						14
						15
						16
						17
						18
						19
						20
						21
						22
						23
						24
						25
						26
						27
						28
						29
						30
						31
						32
						33

Problem 5-15A

Campus Delivery

Work

For Month Ended

	ACCOUNT TITLE	TRIAL BALANCE DEBIT	TRIAL BALANCE CREDIT	ADJUSTMENTS DEBIT	ADJUSTMENTS CREDIT
1	Cash	980 00			
2	Accounts Receivable	590 00			
3	Supplies	575 00			
4	Prepaid Insurance	1,300 00			
5	Van	5,800 00			
6	Accumulated Depreciation—Van				
7	Accounts Payable		960 00		
8	Wages Payable				
9	Jason Armstrong, Capital		10,000 00		
10	Jason Armstrong, Drawing	600 00			
11	Delivery Fees		2,600 00		
12	Wages Expense	1,800 00			
13	Advertising Expense	380 00			
14	Rent Expense	900 00			
15	Supplies Expense				
16	Telephone Expense	220 00			
17	Insurance Expense				
18	Repair Expense	315 00			
19	Oil and Gas Expense	100 00			
20	Depreciation Expense—Van				
21		13,560 00	13,560 00		
22					
23					
24					
25					
26					
27					
28					
29					
30					
31					
32					
33					

Name ______________________________

Problem 5-15A (Concluded)

Service

Sheet

November 30, 20--

ADJUSTED TRIAL BALANCE		INCOME STATEMENT		BALANCE SHEET		
DEBIT	CREDIT	DEBIT	CREDIT	DEBIT	CREDIT	
						1
						2
						3
						4
						5
						6
						7
						8
						9
						10
						11
						12
						13
						14
						15
						16
						17
						18
						19
						20
						21
						22
						23
						24
						25
						26
						27
						28
						29
						30
						31
						32
						33

Problem 5-16A

1. **GENERAL JOURNAL** PAGE 5

	DATE	DESCRIPTION	POST. REF.	DEBIT	CREDIT	
1						1
2						2
3						3
4						4
5						5
6						6
7						7
8						8
9						9
10						10
11						11
12						12
13						13
14						14
15						15
16						16
17						17
18						18
19						19
20						20
21						21
22						22
23						23
24						24
25						25
26						26
27						27
28						28
29						29
30						30
31						31
32						32
33						33
34						34
35						35
36						36

Problem 5-16A (Continued)

2. GENERAL LEDGER

ACCOUNT Supplies ACCOUNT NO. 141

DATE		ITEM	POST. REF.	DEBIT	CREDIT	BALANCE DEBIT	BALANCE CREDIT
20-- Nov.	1		J1	475 00		475 00	
	15		J4	100 00		575 00	

ACCOUNT Prepaid Insurance ACCOUNT NO. 145

DATE		ITEM	POST. REF.	DEBIT	CREDIT	BALANCE DEBIT	BALANCE CREDIT
20-- Nov.	1		J1	1,300 00		1,300 00	

ACCOUNT Accumulated Depreciation—Van ACCOUNT NO. 185.1

DATE		ITEM	POST. REF.	DEBIT	CREDIT	BALANCE DEBIT	BALANCE CREDIT

ACCOUNT Wages Payable ACCOUNT NO. 219

DATE		ITEM	POST. REF.	DEBIT	CREDIT	BALANCE DEBIT	BALANCE CREDIT

Problem 5-16A (Concluded)

GENERAL LEDGER

ACCOUNT Wages Expense ACCOUNT NO. 511

DATE		ITEM	POST. REF.	DEBIT	CREDIT	BALANCE DEBIT	BALANCE CREDIT
20-- Nov.	15		J3	900 00		900 00	
	26		J4	900 00		1800 00	

ACCOUNT Supplies Expense ACCOUNT NO. 523

DATE		ITEM	POST. REF.	DEBIT	CREDIT	BALANCE DEBIT	BALANCE CREDIT

ACCOUNT Insurance Expense ACCOUNT NO. 535

DATE		ITEM	POST. REF.	DEBIT	CREDIT	BALANCE DEBIT	BALANCE CREDIT

ACCOUNT Depreciation Expense—Van ACCOUNT NO. 541

DATE		ITEM	POST. REF.	DEBIT	CREDIT	BALANCE DEBIT	BALANCE CREDIT

Problem 5-17A: See pages 130 and 131

Exercise 5-1B

(Balance Sheet) Supplies		(Income Statement) Supplies Expense	

GENERAL JOURNAL PAGE

	DATE		DESCRIPTION	POST. REF.	DEBIT	CREDIT	
1							1
2							2
3							3
4							4
5							5
6							6

Exercise 5-2B

(Balance Sheet) Prepaid Insurance		(Income Statement) Insurance Expense	

GENERAL JOURNAL PAGE

	DATE		DESCRIPTION	POST. REF.	DEBIT	CREDIT	
1							1
2							2
3							3
4							4
5							5
6							6

Problem 5-17A

Joyce Lee's

Work

For Month Ended

	ACCOUNT TITLE	TRIAL BALANCE DEBIT	TRIAL BALANCE CREDIT	ADJUSTMENTS DEBIT	ADJUSTMENTS CREDIT
1	Cash	1 7 2 5 00			
2	Accounts Receivable	9 6 0 00			
3	Supplies	5 2 5 00			
4	Prepaid Insurance	9 3 0 00			
5	Office Equipment	5 4 5 0 00			
6	Accum. Depr.—Office Equipment				
7	Accounts Payable		4 8 0 00		
8	Wages Payable				
9	Joyce Lee, Capital		7 5 0 0 00		
10	Joyce Lee, Drawing	1 1 2 5 00			
11	Professional Fees		5 7 0 0 00		
12	Wages Expense	1 4 2 0 00			
13	Advertising Expense	3 5 0 00			
14	Rent Expense	7 0 0 00			
15	Supplies Expense				
16	Telephone Expense	1 3 0 00			
17	Utilities Expense	1 9 0 00			
18	Insurance Expense				
19	Depr. Expense—Office Equipment				
20	Miscellaneous Expense	1 7 5 00			
21		13 6 8 0 00	13 6 8 0 00		
22					
23					
24					
25					
26					
27					
28					
29					
30					
31					

Problem 5-17A (Concluded)

Tax Service

Sheet

March 31, 20--

ADJUSTED TRIAL BALANCE		INCOME STATEMENT		BALANCE SHEET		
DEBIT	CREDIT	DEBIT	CREDIT	DEBIT	CREDIT	
						1
						2
						3
						4
						5
						6
						7
						8
						9
						10
						11
						12
						13
						14
						15
						16
						17
						18
						19
						20
						21
						22
						23
						24
						25
						26
						27
						28
						29
						30
						31

Exercise 5-3B

(Income Statement)
Wages Expense

(Balance Sheet)
Wages Payable

GENERAL JOURNAL PAGE

	DATE		DESCRIPTION	POST. REF.	DEBIT	CREDIT	
1							1
2							2
3							3
4							4

Exercise 5-4B

(Income Statement)
Depr. Expense—Delivery Equipment

(Balance Sheet)
Accum. Depr.—Delivery Equipment

GENERAL JOURNAL PAGE

	DATE		DESCRIPTION	POST. REF.	DEBIT	CREDIT	
1							1
2							2
3							3
4							4

Exercise 5-5B

Name ______________________________

Exercise 5-6B

1.

(Balance Sheet) Supplies		(Income Statement) Supplies Expense	
TB 540			
Bal. ______			

2.

(Balance Sheet) Supplies		(Income Statement) Supplies Expense	
TB 330			
Bal. ______			

Exercise 5-7B

1.

(Balance Sheet) Prepaid Insurance		(Income Statement) Insurance Expense	
TB 960			
Bal. ______			

2.

(Balance Sheet) Prepaid Insurance		(Income Statement) Insurance Expense	
TB 1,135			
Bal. ______			

Exercise 5-8B

GENERAL JOURNAL

PAGE 7

DATE		DESCRIPTION	POST. REF.	DEBIT	CREDIT
		Adjusting Entries			
20-- July	31	Insurance Expense		320 00	
		Prepaid Insurance			320 00
	31	Depreciation Expense—Cleaning Equipment		145 00	
		Accumulated Depreciation—Cleaning Equipment			145 00

Exercise 5-8B (Concluded)

GENERAL LEDGER

ACCOUNT Prepaid Insurance ACCOUNT NO. 145

DATE		ITEM	POST. REF.	DEBIT	CREDIT	BALANCE DEBIT	BALANCE CREDIT
20-- July	1	Balance	✓			320 00	
	15		J6	640 00		960 00	

ACCOUNT Accumulated Depreciation—Cleaning Equipment ACCOUNT NO. 183.1

DATE		ITEM	POST. REF.	DEBIT	CREDIT	BALANCE DEBIT	BALANCE CREDIT
20-- July	1	Balance	✓				870 00

ACCOUNT Insurance Expense ACCOUNT NO. 535

DATE		ITEM	POST. REF.	DEBIT	CREDIT	BALANCE DEBIT	BALANCE CREDIT

ACCOUNT Depreciation Expense—Cleaning Equipment ACCOUNT NO. 541

DATE		ITEM	POST. REF.	DEBIT	CREDIT	BALANCE DEBIT	BALANCE CREDIT

Exercise 5-9B

Jasmine Kah's Auto Detailing
Work Sheet (Partial)
For Month Ended June 30, 20--

	ACCOUNT TITLE	TRIAL BALANCE		ADJUSTMENTS		ADJUSTED TRIAL BALANCE		
		DEBIT	CREDIT	DEBIT	CREDIT	DEBIT	CREDIT	
1	Cash	150.00				150.00		1
2	Supplies	520.00				90.00		2
3	Prepaid Insurance	750.00				200.00		3
4	Cleaning Equipment	5,400.00				5,400.00		4
5	Accum. Depr.—Cleaning Equip.		850.00				1,150.00	5
6	Wages Payable						250.00	6
7	Jasmine Kah, Capital		4,600.00				4,600.00	7
8	Detailing Fees		2,220.00				2,220.00	8
9	Wages Expense	700.00				950.00		9
10	Advertising Expense	150.00				150.00		10
11	Supplies Expense					430.00		11
12	Insurance Expense					550.00		12
13	Depr. Exp.—Cleaning Equip.					300.00		13
14		7,670.00	7,670.00			8,220.00	8,220.00	14
15								15
16								16
17								17
18								18
19								19
20								20
21								21
22								22
23								23
24								24
25								25

Name ______________________________

Exercise 5-10B

GENERAL JOURNAL

PAGE

	DATE		DESCRIPTION	POST. REF.	DEBIT	CREDIT	
1							1
2							2
3							3
4							4
5							5
6							6
7							7
8							8
9							9
10							10
11							11
12							12
13							13
14							14
15							15

Exercise 5-11B

	Income Statement Debit	Income Statement Credit	Balance Sheet Debit	Balance Sheet Credit
Cash				
Accounts Receivable				
Supplies				
Prepaid Insurance				
Automobile				
Accum. Depr.—Automobile				
Accounts Payable				
Wages Payable				
Owner, Capital				
Owner, Drawing				
Service Fees				
Wages Expense				
Supplies Expense				
Utilities Expense				
Insurance Expense				
Depr. Exp.—Automobile				

Exercise 5-12B

	Income Statement Debit	Income Statement Credit	Balance Sheet Debit	Balance Sheet Credit
Net Income				
Net Loss				

Name ______________________________

Exercise 5-13B

	Cash Basis	Modified Cash Basis	Accrual Basis
1. Office Equipment Cash Purchased equipment for cash			
2. Office Equipment Accounts Payable Purchased equipment on account			
3. Cash Revenue Cash receipts for week			
4. Accounts Receivable Revenue Services performed on account			
5. Prepaid Insurance Cash Purchased prepaid asset			
6. Supplies Accounts Payable Purchased prepaid asset			
7. Telephone Expense Cash Paid telephone bill			
8. Wages Expense Cash Paid wages for month			
9. Accounts Payable Cash Made payment on account			
10. Supplies Expense Supplies			

Exercise 5-13B (Concluded)

	Cash Basis	Modified Cash Basis	Accrual Basis
11. Wages Expense Wages Payable			
12. Depreciation Expense—Office Equipment Accum. Depr.—Office Equipment			

This page intentionally left blank.

Problem 5-14B

Louie's Lawn

Work

For Month Ended

	ACCOUNT TITLE	TRIAL BALANCE DEBIT	TRIAL BALANCE CREDIT	ADJUSTMENTS DEBIT	ADJUSTMENTS CREDIT
1	Cash	1375 00			
2	Accounts Receivable	880 00			
3	Supplies	490 00			
4	Prepaid Insurance	800 00			
5	Lawn Equipment	5700 00			
6	Accum. Depr.—Lawn Equipment				
7	Accounts Payable		780 00		
8	Wages Payable				
9	Louie Long, Capital		6500 00		
10	Louie Long, Drawing	1250 00			
11	Lawn Service Fees		6100 00		
12	Wages Expense	1145 00			
13	Advertising Expense	540 00			
14	Rent Expense	725 00			
15	Supplies Expense				
16	Telephone Expense	160 00			
17	Insurance Expense				
18	Repair Expense	250 00			
19	Depr. Expense—Lawn Equipment				
20	Miscellaneous Expense	65 00			
21		13380 00	13380 00		
22					
23					
24					
25					
26					
27					
28					
29					
30					
31					
32					
33					

Problem 5-14B (Concluded)

Service

Sheet

March 31, 20--

ADJUSTED TRIAL BALANCE		INCOME STATEMENT		BALANCE SHEET		
DEBIT	CREDIT	DEBIT	CREDIT	DEBIT	CREDIT	
						1
						2
						3
						4
						5
						6
						7
						8
						9
						10
						11
						12
						13
						14
						15
						16
						17
						18
						19
						20
						21
						22
						23
						24
						25
						26
						27
						28
						29
						30
						31
						32
						33

Problem 5-15B

Nolan's Home

Work

For Month Ended

	ACCOUNT TITLE	TRIAL BALANCE DEBIT	TRIAL BALANCE CREDIT	ADJUSTMENTS DEBIT	ADJUSTMENTS CREDIT
1	Cash	830 00			
2	Accounts Receivable	760 00			
3	Supplies	625 00			
4	Prepaid Insurance	950 00			
5	Automobile	6,500 00			
6	Accum. Depr.—Automobile				
7	Accounts Payable		1,500 00		
8	Wages Payable				
9	Val Nolan, Capital		9,900 00		
10	Val Nolan, Drawing	1,100 00			
11	Appraisal Fees		3,000 00		
12	Wages Expense	1,560 00			
13	Advertising Expense	420 00			
14	Rent Expense	1,050 00			
15	Supplies Expense				
16	Telephone Expense	255 00			
17	Insurance Expense				
18	Repair Expense	270 00			
19	Oil and Gas Expense	80 00			
20	Depr. Expense—Automobile				
21		14,400 00	14,400 00		
22					
23					
24					
25					
26					
27					
28					
29					
30					
31					
32					
33					

Name ______________________________

Problem 5-15B (Concluded)

Appraisals

Sheet

October 31, 20--

ADJUSTED TRIAL BALANCE		INCOME STATEMENT		BALANCE SHEET		
DEBIT	CREDIT	DEBIT	CREDIT	DEBIT	CREDIT	
						1
						2
						3
						4
						5
						6
						7
						8
						9
						10
						11
						12
						13
						14
						15
						16
						17
						18
						19
						20
						21
						22
						23
						24
						25
						26
						27
						28
						29
						30
						31
						32
						33

Problem 5-16B

1.

GENERAL JOURNAL

PAGE 3

	DATE		DESCRIPTION	POST. REF.	DEBIT	CREDIT	
1							1
2							2
3							3
4							4
5							5
6							6
7							7
8							8
9							9
10							10
11							11
12							12
13							13
14							14
15							15
16							16
17							17
18							18
19							19
20							20
21							21
22							22
23							23
24							24
25							25
26							26
27							27
28							28
29							29
30							30
31							31
32							32
33							33
34							34
35							35
36							36

Problem 5-16B (Continued)

2.

GENERAL LEDGER

ACCOUNT Supplies ACCOUNT NO. 141

DATE		ITEM	POST. REF.	DEBIT	CREDIT	BALANCE DEBIT	BALANCE CREDIT
20-- Oct.	2		J1	625 00		625 00	

ACCOUNT Prepaid Insurance ACCOUNT NO. 145

DATE		ITEM	POST. REF.	DEBIT	CREDIT	BALANCE DEBIT	BALANCE CREDIT
20-- Oct.	3		J1	950 00		950 00	

ACCOUNT Accumulated Depreciation—Automobile ACCOUNT NO. 185.1

DATE		ITEM	POST. REF.	DEBIT	CREDIT	BALANCE DEBIT	BALANCE CREDIT

Problem 5-16B (Continued)

ACCOUNT Wages Payable ACCOUNT NO. 219

DATE		ITEM	POST. REF.	DEBIT	CREDIT	BALANCE DEBIT	BALANCE CREDIT

ACCOUNT Wages Expense ACCOUNT NO. 511

DATE		ITEM	POST. REF.	DEBIT	CREDIT	BALANCE DEBIT	BALANCE CREDIT
20-- Oct.	15		J2	700 00		700 00	
	26		J2	860 00		1560 00	

ACCOUNT Supplies Expense ACCOUNT NO. 523

DATE		ITEM	POST. REF.	DEBIT	CREDIT	BALANCE DEBIT	BALANCE CREDIT

Problem 5-16B (Concluded)

ACCOUNT Insurance Expense ACCOUNT NO. 535

DATE		ITEM	POST. REF.	DEBIT	CREDIT	BALANCE	
						DEBIT	CREDIT

ACCOUNT Depreciation Expense—Automobile ACCOUNT NO. 541

DATE		ITEM	POST. REF.	DEBIT	CREDIT	BALANCE	
						DEBIT	CREDIT

Problem 5-17B

Dick Ady's

Work

For Month Ended

	ACCOUNT TITLE	TRIAL BALANCE DEBIT	TRIAL BALANCE CREDIT	ADJUSTMENTS DEBIT	ADJUSTMENTS CREDIT
1	Cash	1 3 6 5 00			
2	Accounts Receivable	8 4 5 00			
3	Supplies	6 2 0 00			
4	Prepaid Insurance	1 1 5 0 00			
5	Office Equipment	6 4 0 0 00			
6	Accum. Depr.—Office Equipment				
7	Accounts Payable		7 3 5 00		
8	Wages Payable				
9	Dick Ady, Capital		7 8 0 0 00		
10	Dick Ady, Drawing	1 2 0 0 00			
11	Professional Fees		6 3 5 0 00		
12	Wages Expense	1 4 9 5 00			
13	Advertising Expense	3 8 0 00			
14	Rent Expense	8 5 0 00			
15	Supplies Expense				
16	Telephone Expense	2 0 5 00			
17	Utilities Expense	2 8 5 00			
18	Insurance Expense				
19	Depr. Expense—Office Equipment				
20	Miscellaneous Expense	9 0 00			
21		14 8 8 5 00	14 8 8 5 00		
22					
23					
24					
25					
26					
27					
28					
29					
30					
31					
32					

Problem 5-17B (Concluded)

Bookkeeping Service

Sheet

July 31, 20--

ADJUSTED TRIAL BALANCE		INCOME STATEMENT		BALANCE SHEET		
DEBIT	CREDIT	DEBIT	CREDIT	DEBIT	CREDIT	
						1
						2
						3
						4
						5
						6
						7
						8
						9
						10
						11
						12
						13
						14
						15
						16
						17
						18
						19
						20
						21
						22
						23
						24
						25
						26
						27
						28
						29
						30
						31
						32

Mastery Problem

1.

Kristi Williams Family

Work

For Year Ended

	ACCOUNT TITLE	TRIAL BALANCE DEBIT	TRIAL BALANCE CREDIT	ADJUSTMENTS DEBIT	ADJUSTMENTS CREDIT
1	Cash	8730 00			
2	Office Supplies	700 00			
3	Prepaid Insurance	600 00			
4	Office Equipment	18000 00			
5					
6	Computer Equipment	6000 00			
7					
8	Notes Payable		8000 00		
9	Accounts Payable		500 00		
10	Kristi Williams, Capital		11400 00		
11	Kristi Williams, Drawing	3000 00			
12	Client Fees		35800 00		
13	Wages Expense	9500 00			
14	Rent Expense	6000 00			
15					
16	Utilities Expense	2170 00			
17					
18					
19					
20	Miscellaneous Expense	1000 00			
21		55700 00	55700 00		
22					
23					
24					
25					
26					
27					
28					
29					
30					
31					
32					

Mastery Problem (Continued)

Counseling Services

Sheet

December 31, 20--

ADJUSTED TRIAL BALANCE		INCOME STATEMENT		BALANCE SHEET	
DEBIT	CREDIT	DEBIT	CREDIT	DEBIT	CREDIT

Mastery Problem (Concluded)

2.

GENERAL JOURNAL

PAGE

DATE		DESCRIPTION	POST. REF.	DEBIT	CREDIT

Name ______________________________

Challenge Problem

See pages 156–157 for work sheet for Challenge Problem.

Challenge Problem

1.

Diane Kiefner's Wilderness

Work

For Summer

	ACCOUNT TITLE	TRIAL BALANCE DEBIT	TRIAL BALANCE CREDIT	ADJUSTMENTS DEBIT	ADJUSTMENTS CREDIT
1	Cash	11 5 0 0 00			
2					
3					
4					
5	Diane Kiefner, Capital		15 0 0 0 00		
6	Tour Revenue		10 0 0 0 00		
7	Advertising Supplies Expense	1 0 0 0 00			
8	Food Expense	2 0 0 0 00			
9	Equipment Rental Expense	3 0 0 0 00			
10	Travel Expense	4 0 0 0 00			
11	Kayak Expense	3 5 0 0 00			
12					
13		25 0 0 0 00	25 0 0 0 00		
14					
15					
16					
17					
18					
19					

Challenge Problem (Concluded)

Kayaking Tours

Sheet

Ended 20--

ADJUSTED TRIAL BALANCE		INCOME STATEMENT		BALANCE SHEET		
DEBIT	CREDIT	DEBIT	CREDIT	DEBIT	CREDIT	
						1
						2
						3
						4
						5
						6
						7
						8
						9
						10
						11
						12
						13
						14
						15
						16
						17
						18
						19

2.

APPENDIX: DEPRECIATION METHODS

Exercise 5Apx-1A

Straight-Line Depreciation

Year	Depreciable Cost	×	Rate	=	Depreciation Expense	Accumulated Depreciation End of Year	Book Value End of Year

Exercise 5Apx-2A

Sum-of-the-Years'-Digits

Year	Depreciable Cost	×	Rate	=	Depreciation Expense	Accumulated Depreciation End of Year	Book Value End of Year

Exercise 5Apx-3A

Double-Declining-Balance Method

Year	Book Value Beginning of Year	×	Rate	=	Depreciation Expense	Accumulated Depreciation End of Year	Book Value End of Year

Exercise 5Apx-4A

Modified Accelerated Cost Recovery System

Year	Cost	×	Rate	=	Depreciation Expense	Accumulated Depreciation End of Year	Book Value End of Year

Exercise 5Apx-1B

Straight-Line Depreciation

Year	Depreciable Cost	×	Rate	=	Depreciation Expense	Accumulated Depreciation End of Year	Book Value End of Year

Exercise 5Apx-2B

Sum-of-the-Years'-Digits

Year	Depreciable Cost	×	Rate	=	Depreciation Expense	Accumulated Depreciation End of Year	Book Value End of Year

Exercise 5Apx-3B

Double-Declining-Balance Method

Year	Book Value Beginning of Year	×	Rate	=	Depreciation Expense	Accumulated Depreciation End of Year	Book Value End of Year

Exercise 5Apx-4B

Modified Accelerated Cost Recovery System

Year	Cost	×	Rate	=	Depreciation Expense	Accumulated Depreciation End of Year	Book Value End of Year

Name ______________________________

Exercise 6-1A

Exercise 6-2A

Exercise 6-3A

Name ______________________________

Exercise 6-4A

GENERAL JOURNAL

PAGE 1

	DATE		DESCRIPTION	POST. REF.	DEBIT	CREDIT	
1							1
2							2
3							3
4							4
5							5
6							6
7							7
8							8
9							9
10							10
11							11
12							12
13							13
14							14
15							15
16							16
17							17
18							18
19							19
20							20
21							21
22							22
23							23

Exercise 6-4A (Concluded)

Name ______________________________

Exercise 6-5A

GENERAL JOURNAL

PAGE

	DATE		DESCRIPTION	POST. REF.	DEBIT	CREDIT	
1							1
2							2
3							3
4							4
5							5
6							6
7							7
8							8
9							9
10							10
11							11
12							12
13							13
14							14
15							15
16							16
17							17
18							18
19							19
20							20
21							21
22							22
23							23
24							24
25							25
26							26
27							27
28							28
29							29
30							30
31							31
32							32
33							33
34							34
35							35
36							36

Exercise 6-5A (Concluded)

Cash — 101

Debit		Credit	
Bal.	500		

Accounts Receivable — 122

Debit		Credit	
Bal.	1,500		

Wages Payable — 219

Debit		Credit	
		Bal.	400

Chris Williams, Capital — 311

Debit		Credit	
		Bal.	9,000

Chris Williams, Drawing — 312

Debit		Credit	
Bal.	1,000		

Income Summary — 313

Debit		Credit	

Golf Instruction Fees — 401

Debit		Credit	
		Bal.	4,000

Wages Expense — 511

Debit		Credit	
Bal.	800		

Advertising Expense — 512

Debit		Credit	
Bal.	200		

Travel Expense — 515

Debit		Credit	
Bal.	600		

Supplies Expense — 524

Debit		Credit	
Bal.	500		

Insurance Expense — 535

Debit		Credit	
Bal.	100		

Postage Expense — 536

Debit		Credit	
Bal.	50		

Gas and Oil Expense — 538

Debit		Credit	
Bal.	150		

Miscellaneous Expense — 549

Debit		Credit	
Bal.	80		

Name ______________________________

Exercise 6-6A

GENERAL JOURNAL

PAGE

	DATE		DESCRIPTION	POST. REF.	DEBIT	CREDIT	
1							1
2							2
3							3
4							4
5							5
6							6
7							7
8							8
9							9
10							10
11							11
12							12
13							13
14							14
15							15
16							16
17							17
18							18
19							19
20							20
21							21
22							22
23							23
24							24
25							25
26							26
27							27
28							28
29							29
30							30
31							31
32							32
33							33
34							34
35							35
36							36

Exercise 6-6A (Concluded)

Accum. Depr.—Delivery Equip. 185.1

Debit		Credit	
		Bal.	100

Wages Payable 219

Debit		Credit	
		Bal.	200

Saburo Goto, Capital 311

Debit		Credit	
		Bal.	4,000

Saburo Goto, Drawing 312

Debit		Credit	
Bal.	800		

Income Summary 313

Debit		Credit	

Delivery Fees 401

Debit		Credit	
		Bal.	2,200

Wages Expense 511

Debit		Credit	
Bal.	1,800		

Advertising Expense 512

Debit		Credit	
Bal.	80		

Rent Expense 521

Debit		Credit	
Bal.	500		

Supplies Expense 523

Debit		Credit	
Bal.	120		

Telephone Expense 525

Debit		Credit	
Bal.	58		

Electricity Expense 533

Debit		Credit	
Bal.	44		

Insurance Expense 535

Debit		Credit	
Bal.	30		

Gas and Oil Expense 538

Debit		Credit	
Bal.	38		

Depr. Exp.—Delivery Equip. 541

Debit		Credit	
Bal.	100		

Miscellaneous Expense 549

Debit		Credit	
Bal.	33		

Problem 6-7A

1.

2.

Problem 6-7A (Concluded)

3.

Name ______________________________

Problem 6-8A

1.

GENERAL JOURNAL

PAGE 10

	DATE		DESCRIPTION	POST. REF.	DEBIT	CREDIT	
1							1
2							2
3							3
4							4
5							5
6							6
7							7
8							8
9							9
10							10
11							11
12							12
13							13
14							14
15							15
16							16
17							17
18							18

Problem 6-8A (Continued)

2.

GENERAL JOURNAL

PAGE 11

	DATE		DESCRIPTION	POST. REF.	DEBIT	CREDIT	
1							1
2							2
3							3
4							4
5							5
6							6
7							7
8							8
9							9
10							10
11							11
12							12
13							13
14							14
15							15
16							16
17							17
18							18
19							19
20							20
21							21
22							22
23							23

1. and 2.

GENERAL LEDGER

ACCOUNT Cash ACCOUNT NO. 101

DATE		ITEM	POST. REF.	DEBIT	CREDIT	BALANCE	
						DEBIT	CREDIT
20-- Jan.	31	Balance	✓			3,673.00	

Problem 6-8A (Continued)

ACCOUNT Accounts Receivable ACCOUNT NO. 122

DATE		ITEM	POST. REF.	DEBIT	CREDIT	BALANCE DEBIT	BALANCE CREDIT
20-- Jan.	31	Balance	✓			1 4 5 0 00	

ACCOUNT Supplies ACCOUNT NO. 141

DATE		ITEM	POST. REF.	DEBIT	CREDIT	BALANCE DEBIT	BALANCE CREDIT
20-- Jan.	31	Balance	✓			7 0 0 00	

ACCOUNT Prepaid Insurance ACCOUNT NO. 145

DATE		ITEM	POST. REF.	DEBIT	CREDIT	BALANCE DEBIT	BALANCE CREDIT
20-- Jan.	31	Balance	✓			9 0 0 00	

ACCOUNT Delivery Equipment ACCOUNT NO. 185

DATE		ITEM	POST. REF.	DEBIT	CREDIT	BALANCE DEBIT	BALANCE CREDIT
20-- Jan.	31	Balance	✓			3 2 0 0 00	

ACCOUNT Accumulated Depreciation—Delivery Equipment ACCOUNT NO. 185.1

DATE		ITEM	POST. REF.	DEBIT	CREDIT	BALANCE DEBIT	BALANCE CREDIT

Problem 6-8A (Continued)

ACCOUNT Accounts Payable ACCOUNT NO. 202

DATE		ITEM	POST. REF.	DEBIT	CREDIT	BALANCE DEBIT	BALANCE CREDIT
20-- Jan.	31	Balance	✓				12,000 00

ACCOUNT Wages Payable ACCOUNT NO. 219

DATE		ITEM	POST. REF.	DEBIT	CREDIT	BALANCE DEBIT	BALANCE CREDIT

ACCOUNT Don Megaffin, Capital ACCOUNT NO. 311

DATE		ITEM	POST. REF.	DEBIT	CREDIT	BALANCE DEBIT	BALANCE CREDIT
20-- Jan.	31	Balance	✓				8,000 00

ACCOUNT Don Megaffin, Drawing ACCOUNT NO. 312

DATE		ITEM	POST. REF.	DEBIT	CREDIT	BALANCE DEBIT	BALANCE CREDIT
20-- Jan.	31	Balance	✓			11,000 00	

ACCOUNT Income Summary ACCOUNT NO. 313

DATE		ITEM	POST. REF.	DEBIT	CREDIT	BALANCE DEBIT	BALANCE CREDIT

Name ____________________

Problem 6-8A (Continued)

ACCOUNT Repair Fees ACCOUNT NO. 401

DATE		ITEM	POST. REF.	DEBIT	CREDIT	BALANCE DEBIT	BALANCE CREDIT
20-- Jan.	31	Balance	✓				4,700 00

ACCOUNT Wages Expense ACCOUNT NO. 511

DATE		ITEM	POST. REF.	DEBIT	CREDIT	BALANCE DEBIT	BALANCE CREDIT
20-- Jan.	31	Balance	✓			1,750 00	

ACCOUNT Advertising Expense ACCOUNT NO. 512

DATE		ITEM	POST. REF.	DEBIT	CREDIT	BALANCE DEBIT	BALANCE CREDIT
20-- Jan.	31	Balance	✓			200 00	

ACCOUNT Rent Expense ACCOUNT NO. 521

DATE		ITEM	POST. REF.	DEBIT	CREDIT	BALANCE DEBIT	BALANCE CREDIT
20-- Jan.	31	Balance	✓			640 00	

ACCOUNT Supplies Expense ACCOUNT NO. 523

DATE		ITEM	POST. REF.	DEBIT	CREDIT	BALANCE DEBIT	BALANCE CREDIT

Problem 6-8A (Continued)

ACCOUNT Telephone Expense — ACCOUNT NO. 525

DATE		ITEM	POST. REF.	DEBIT	CREDIT	BALANCE DEBIT	BALANCE CREDIT
20-- Jan.	31	Balance	✓			50 00	

ACCOUNT Insurance Expense — ACCOUNT NO. 535

DATE		ITEM	POST. REF.	DEBIT	CREDIT	BALANCE DEBIT	BALANCE CREDIT

ACCOUNT Gas and Oil Expense — ACCOUNT NO. 538

DATE		ITEM	POST. REF.	DEBIT	CREDIT	BALANCE DEBIT	BALANCE CREDIT
20-- Jan.	31	Balance	✓			200 00	

ACCOUNT Depreciation Expense—Delivery Equipment — ACCOUNT NO. 541

DATE		ITEM	POST. REF.	DEBIT	CREDIT	BALANCE DEBIT	BALANCE CREDIT

ACCOUNT Miscellaneous Expense — ACCOUNT NO. 549

DATE		ITEM	POST. REF.	DEBIT	CREDIT	BALANCE DEBIT	BALANCE CREDIT
20-- Jan.	31	Balance	✓			37 00	

Problem 6-8A (Concluded)

3.

ACCOUNT TITLE	ACCT. NO.	DEBIT BALANCE	CREDIT BALANCE

Problem 6-9A

Exercise 6-1B

Exercise 6-2B

Name ______________________________

Exercise 6-3B

Exercise 6-4B

GENERAL JOURNAL

PAGE 1

	DATE		DESCRIPTION	POST. REF.	DEBIT	CREDIT	
1							1
2							2
3							3
4							4
5							5
6							6
7							7
8							8
9							9
10							10
11							11
12							12
13							13
14							14
15							15
16							16
17							17
18							18
19							19
20							20
21							21
22							22
23							23

Exercise 6-4B (Concluded)

Exercise 6-5B

GENERAL JOURNAL

PAGE

	DATE		DESCRIPTION	POST. REF.	DEBIT	CREDIT	
1							1
2							2
3							3
4							4
5							5
6							6
7							7
8							8
9							9
10							10
11							11
12							12
13							13
14							14
15							15
16							16
17							17
18							18
19							19
20							20
21							21
22							22
23							23
24							24
25							25
26							26
27							27
28							28
29							29
30							30
31							31
32							32
33							33
34							34
35							35
36							36

Exercise 6-5B (Concluded)

Cash 101

Bal.	600		

Accounts Receivable 122

Bal.	1,800		

Wages Payable 219

		Bal.	500

Mark Thrasher, Capital 311

		Bal.	8,000

Mark Thrasher, Drawing 312

Bal.	800		

Income Summary 313

Lawn Service Fees 401

		Bal.	5,000

Wages Expense 511

Bal.	400		

Advertising Expense 512

Bal.	600		

Travel Expense 515

Bal.	100		

Supplies Expense 524

Bal.	900		

Insurance Expense 535

Bal.	300		

Postage Expense 536

Bal.	40		

Gas and Oil Expense 538

Bal.	700		

Miscellaneous Expense 549

Bal.	200		

Exercise 6-6B

GENERAL JOURNAL

PAGE

DATE		DESCRIPTION	POST. REF.	DEBIT	CREDIT

Exercise 6-6B (Concluded)

Accum. Depr.—Office Equip. 181.1

		Bal.	110

Wages Payable 219

		Bal.	260

Raquel Zapata, Capital 311

		Bal.	6,000

Raquel Zapata, Drawing 312

Bal.	2,000		

Income Summary 313

Referral Fees 401

		Bal.	2,813

Wages Expense 511

Bal.	1,080		

Advertising Expense 512

Bal.	34		

Rent Expense 521

Bal.	900		

Supplies Expense 523

Bal.	322		

Telephone Expense 525

Bal.	133		

Utilities Expense 533

Bal.	102		

Insurance Expense 535

Bal.	120		

Gas and Oil Expense 538

Bal.	88		

Depr. Exp.—Office Equip. 541

Bal.	110		

Miscellaneous Expense 549

Bal.	98		

Problem 6-7B

1.

2.

Name ______________________________

Problem 6-7B (Concluded)

3.

Problem 6-8B

1.

GENERAL JOURNAL

PAGE 10

	DATE		DESCRIPTION	POST. REF.	DEBIT	CREDIT	
1							1
2							2
3							3
4							4
5							5
6							6
7							7
8							8
9							9
10							10
11							11
12							12
13							13
14							14
15							15
16							16
17							17
18							18

Problem 6-8B (Continued)

2.

GENERAL JOURNAL

PAGE 11

	DATE		DESCRIPTION	POST. REF.	DEBIT	CREDIT	
1							1
2							2
3							3
4							4
5							5
6							6
7							7
8							8
9							9
10							10
11							11
12							12
13							13
14							14
15							15
16							16
17							17
18							18
19							19
20							20
21							21
22							22
23							23

1. and 2.

GENERAL LEDGER

ACCOUNT Cash ACCOUNT NO. 101

DATE		ITEM	POST. REF.	DEBIT	CREDIT	BALANCE DEBIT	BALANCE CREDIT
20-- June	30	Balance	✓			5,285.00	

Problem 6-8B (Continued)

ACCOUNT Accounts Receivable — ACCOUNT NO. 122

DATE		ITEM	POST. REF.	DEBIT	CREDIT	BALANCE DEBIT	BALANCE CREDIT
20-- June	30	Balance	✓			1 0 7 5 00	

ACCOUNT Supplies — ACCOUNT NO. 141

DATE		ITEM	POST. REF.	DEBIT	CREDIT	BALANCE DEBIT	BALANCE CREDIT
20-- June	30	Balance	✓			7 5 0 00	

ACCOUNT Prepaid Insurance — ACCOUNT NO. 145

DATE		ITEM	POST. REF.	DEBIT	CREDIT	BALANCE DEBIT	BALANCE CREDIT
20-- June	30	Balance	✓			5 0 0 00	

ACCOUNT Office Equipment — ACCOUNT NO. 181

DATE		ITEM	POST. REF.	DEBIT	CREDIT	BALANCE DEBIT	BALANCE CREDIT
20-- June	30	Balance	✓			2 2 0 0 00	

ACCOUNT Accumulated Depreciation—Office Equipment — ACCOUNT NO. 181.1

DATE		ITEM	POST. REF.	DEBIT	CREDIT	BALANCE DEBIT	BALANCE CREDIT

Name ______________________________

Problem 6-8B (Continued)

ACCOUNT Accounts Payable ACCOUNT NO. 202

DATE		ITEM	POST. REF.	DEBIT	CREDIT	BALANCE DEBIT	BALANCE CREDIT
20-- June	30	Balance	✓				1,500 00

ACCOUNT Wages Payable ACCOUNT NO. 219

DATE		ITEM	POST. REF.	DEBIT	CREDIT	BALANCE DEBIT	BALANCE CREDIT

ACCOUNT Juanita Alvarez, Capital ACCOUNT NO. 311

DATE		ITEM	POST. REF.	DEBIT	CREDIT	BALANCE DEBIT	BALANCE CREDIT
20-- June	30	Balance	✓				7,000 00

ACCOUNT Juanita Alvarez, Drawing ACCOUNT NO. 312

DATE		ITEM	POST. REF.	DEBIT	CREDIT	BALANCE DEBIT	BALANCE CREDIT
20-- June	30	Balance	✓			800 00	

ACCOUNT Income Summary ACCOUNT NO. 313

DATE		ITEM	POST. REF.	DEBIT	CREDIT	BALANCE DEBIT	BALANCE CREDIT

Problem 6-8B (Continued)

ACCOUNT Consulting Fees ACCOUNT NO. 401

DATE		ITEM	POST. REF.	DEBIT	CREDIT	BALANCE DEBIT	BALANCE CREDIT
20-- June	30	Balance	✓				4,204.00

ACCOUNT Wages Expense ACCOUNT NO. 511

DATE		ITEM	POST. REF.	DEBIT	CREDIT	BALANCE DEBIT	BALANCE CREDIT
20-- June	30	Balance	✓			1,400.00	

ACCOUNT Advertising Expense ACCOUNT NO. 512

DATE		ITEM	POST. REF.	DEBIT	CREDIT	BALANCE DEBIT	BALANCE CREDIT
20-- June	30	Balance	✓			60.00	

ACCOUNT Rent Expense ACCOUNT NO. 521

DATE		ITEM	POST. REF.	DEBIT	CREDIT	BALANCE DEBIT	BALANCE CREDIT
20-- June	30	Balance	✓			500.00	

ACCOUNT Supplies Expense ACCOUNT NO. 523

DATE		ITEM	POST. REF.	DEBIT	CREDIT	BALANCE DEBIT	BALANCE CREDIT

Problem 6-8B (Continued)

ACCOUNT Telephone Expense ACCOUNT NO. 525

DATE		ITEM	POST. REF.	DEBIT	CREDIT	BALANCE DEBIT	BALANCE CREDIT
20-- June	30	Balance	✓			46 00	

ACCOUNT Electricity Expense ACCOUNT NO. 533

DATE		ITEM	POST. REF.	DEBIT	CREDIT	BALANCE DEBIT	BALANCE CREDIT
20-- June	30	Balance	✓			39 00	

ACCOUNT Insurance Expense ACCOUNT NO. 535

DATE		ITEM	POST. REF.	DEBIT	CREDIT	BALANCE DEBIT	BALANCE CREDIT

ACCOUNT Gas and Oil Expense ACCOUNT NO. 538

DATE		ITEM	POST. REF.	DEBIT	CREDIT	BALANCE DEBIT	BALANCE CREDIT
20-- June	30	Balance	✓			28 00	

ACCOUNT Depreciation Expense—Office Equipment ACCOUNT NO. 541

DATE		ITEM	POST. REF.	DEBIT	CREDIT	BALANCE DEBIT	BALANCE CREDIT

Problem 6-8B (Concluded)

ACCOUNT Miscellaneous Expense ACCOUNT NO. 549

DATE		ITEM	POST. REF.	DEBIT	CREDIT	BALANCE DEBIT	BALANCE CREDIT
20-- June	30	Balance	✓			2 1 00	

3.

ACCOUNT TITLE	ACCT. NO.	DEBIT BALANCE	CREDIT BALANCE

Problem 6-9B

Mastery Problem

GENERAL JOURNAL

PAGE 4

DATE	DESCRIPTION	POST. REF.	DEBIT	CREDIT

Mastery Problem (Continued)

Mastery Problem (Concluded)

Name ______________________________

Challenge Problem

Challenge Problem (Concluded)

Name ______________________________

Exercise 6Apx-1A

a. ________________

b. ________________

c. ________________

d. ________________

e. ________________

f. ________________

g. ________________

h. ________________

i. ________________

j. ________________

k. ________________

Problem 6Apx-2A

Exercise 6Apx-1B

a. ____________________

b. ____________________

c. ____________________

d. ____________________

e. ____________________

f. ____________________

g. ____________________

h. ____________________

i. ____________________

j. ____________________

k. ____________________

Problem 6Apx-2B

Comprehensive Problem 1: The Accounting Cycle

1.

GENERAL JOURNAL

PAGE 1

	DATE		DESCRIPTION	POST. REF.	DEBIT	CREDIT	
1							1
2							2
3							3
4							4
5							5
6							6
7							7
8							8
9							9
10							10
11							11
12							12
13							13
14							14
15							15
16							16
17							17
18							18
19							19
20							20
21							21
22							22
23							23
24							24
25							25
26							26
27							27
28							28
29							29
30							30
31							31
32							32
33							33
34							34

Comprehensive Problem 1 (Continued)

GENERAL JOURNAL

PAGE 2

DATE	DESCRIPTION	POST. REF.	DEBIT	CREDIT

Comprehensive Problem 1 (Continued)

GENERAL JOURNAL

PAGE 3

	DATE	DESCRIPTION	POST. REF.	DEBIT	CREDIT	
1						1
2						2
3						3
4						4
5						5
6						6
7						7
8						8
9						9
10						10
11						11
12						12
13						13
14						14
15						15
16						16
17						17
18						18
19						19
20						20
21						21
22						22
23						23
24						24
25						25
26						26
27						27
28						28
29						29
30						30
31						31
32						32
33						33
34						34
35						35

Comprehensive Problem 1 (Continued)

GENERAL JOURNAL

PAGE 4

	DATE		DESCRIPTION	POST. REF.	DEBIT	CREDIT	
1							1
2							2
3							3
4							4
5							5
6							6
7							7
8							8
9							9
10							10
11							11

2., 6., and 11.

GENERAL LEDGER

ACCOUNT Cash ACCOUNT NO. 101

DATE		ITEM	POST. REF.	DEBIT	CREDIT	BALANCE	
						DEBIT	CREDIT

Name ______________________________

Comprehensive Problem 1 (Continued)

ACCOUNT Office Supplies ACCOUNT NO. 142

DATE	ITEM	POST. REF.	DEBIT	CREDIT	BALANCE	
					DEBIT	CREDIT

ACCOUNT Food Supplies ACCOUNT NO. 144

DATE	ITEM	POST. REF.	DEBIT	CREDIT	BALANCE	
					DEBIT	CREDIT

ACCOUNT Prepaid Insurance ACCOUNT NO. 145

DATE	ITEM	POST. REF.	DEBIT	CREDIT	BALANCE	
					DEBIT	CREDIT

ACCOUNT Fishing Boats ACCOUNT NO. 181

DATE	ITEM	POST. REF.	DEBIT	CREDIT	BALANCE	
					DEBIT	CREDIT

Comprehensive Problem 1 (Continued)

ACCOUNT Accumulated Depreciation—Fishing Boats ACCOUNT NO. 181.1

DATE	ITEM	POST. REF.	DEBIT	CREDIT	BALANCE DEBIT	BALANCE CREDIT

ACCOUNT Accounts Payable ACCOUNT NO. 202

DATE	ITEM	POST. REF.	DEBIT	CREDIT	BALANCE DEBIT	BALANCE CREDIT

ACCOUNT Wages Payable ACCOUNT NO. 219

DATE	ITEM	POST. REF.	DEBIT	CREDIT	BALANCE DEBIT	BALANCE CREDIT

ACCOUNT Bob Night, Capital ACCOUNT NO. 311

DATE	ITEM	POST. REF.	DEBIT	CREDIT	BALANCE DEBIT	BALANCE CREDIT

Comprehensive Problem 1 (Continued)

ACCOUNT Bob Night, Drawing ACCOUNT NO. 312

DATE		ITEM	POST. REF.	DEBIT	CREDIT	BALANCE DEBIT	BALANCE CREDIT

ACCOUNT Income Summary ACCOUNT NO. 313

DATE		ITEM	POST. REF.	DEBIT	CREDIT	BALANCE DEBIT	BALANCE CREDIT

ACCOUNT Registration Fees ACCOUNT NO. 401

DATE		ITEM	POST. REF.	DEBIT	CREDIT	BALANCE DEBIT	BALANCE CREDIT

Comprehensive Problem 1 (Continued)

ACCOUNT Wages Expense ACCOUNT NO. 511

DATE	ITEM	POST. REF.	DEBIT	CREDIT	BALANCE DEBIT	BALANCE CREDIT

ACCOUNT Rent Expense ACCOUNT NO. 521

DATE	ITEM	POST. REF.	DEBIT	CREDIT	BALANCE DEBIT	BALANCE CREDIT

ACCOUNT Office Supplies Expense ACCOUNT NO. 523

DATE	ITEM	POST. REF.	DEBIT	CREDIT	BALANCE DEBIT	BALANCE CREDIT

ACCOUNT Food Supplies Expense ACCOUNT NO. 524

DATE	ITEM	POST. REF.	DEBIT	CREDIT	BALANCE DEBIT	BALANCE CREDIT

Name ______________________________

Comprehensive Problem 1 (Continued)

ACCOUNT Telephone Expense ACCOUNT NO. 525

DATE		ITEM	POST. REF.	DEBIT	CREDIT	BALANCE DEBIT	BALANCE CREDIT

ACCOUNT Utilities Expense ACCOUNT NO. 533

DATE		ITEM	POST. REF.	DEBIT	CREDIT	BALANCE DEBIT	BALANCE CREDIT

ACCOUNT Insurance Expense ACCOUNT NO. 535

DATE		ITEM	POST. REF.	DEBIT	CREDIT	BALANCE DEBIT	BALANCE CREDIT

ACCOUNT Postage Expense ACCOUNT NO. 536

DATE		ITEM	POST. REF.	DEBIT	CREDIT	BALANCE DEBIT	BALANCE CREDIT

ACCOUNT Depreciation Expense—Fishing Boats ACCOUNT NO. 542

DATE		ITEM	POST. REF.	DEBIT	CREDIT	BALANCE DEBIT	BALANCE CREDIT

Comprehensive Problem 1 (Continued)

3. and 4.

	ACCOUNT TITLE	TRIAL BALANCE		ADJUSTMENTS	
		DEBIT	CREDIT	DEBIT	CREDIT
1					
2					
3					
4					
5					
6					
7					
8					
9					
10					
11					
12					
13					
14					
15					
16					
17					
18					
19					
20					
21					
22					
23					
24					
25					
26					
27					
28					
29					
30					
31					

Comprehensive Problem 1 (Continued)

ADJUSTED TRIAL BALANCE		INCOME STATEMENT		BALANCE SHEET	
DEBIT	CREDIT	DEBIT	CREDIT	DEBIT	CREDIT

Comprehensive Problem 1 (Continued)

7.

8.

Comprehensive Problem 1 (Continued)

9.

Comprehensive Problem 1 (Continued)

5. and 10.

GENERAL JOURNAL

PAGE 5

	DATE		DESCRIPTION	POST. REF.	DEBIT	CREDIT	
1							1
2							2
3							3
4							4
5							5
6							6
7							7
8							8
9							9
10							10
11							11
12							12
13							13
14							14
15							15
16							16
17							17
18							18
19							19
20							20
21							21
22							22
23							23
24							24
25							25
26							26
27							27
28							28
29							29
30							30
31							31
32							32
33							33
34							34
35							35

Comprehensive Problem 1 (Concluded)

GENERAL JOURNAL

PAGE 6

	DATE		DESCRIPTION	POST. REF.	DEBIT	CREDIT	
1							1
2							2
3							3
4							4
5							5
6							6
7							7
8							8
9							9

12.

ACCOUNT	ACCT. NO.	DEBIT BALANCE	CREDIT BALANCE

Comprehensive Problem 1, Period 2: The Accounting Cycle

1.

GENERAL JOURNAL

PAGE 5

	DATE		DESCRIPTION	POST. REF.	DEBIT	CREDIT	
1							1
2							2
3							3
4							4
5							5
6							6
7							7
8							8
9							9
10							10
11							11
12							12
13							13
14							14
15							15
16							16
17							17
18							18
19							19
20							20
21							21
22							22
23							23
24							24
25							25
26							26
27							27
28							28
29							29
30							30
31							31
32							32
33							33
34							34
35							35

Comprehensive Problem 1, Period 2 (Continued)

GENERAL JOURNAL PAGE 6

	DATE		DESCRIPTION	POST. REF.	DEBIT	CREDIT	
1							1
2							2
3							3
4							4
5							5
6							6
7							7
8							8
9							9
10							10
11							11
12							12
13							13
14							14
15							15
16							16
17							17
18							18
19							19
20							20
21							21
22							22
23							23
24							24
25							25
26							26
27							27
28							28
29							29
30							30
31							31
32							32
33							33
34							34
35							35
36							36
37							37
38							38
39							39
40							40
41							41
42							42

Name ______________________________

Comprehensive Problem 1, Period 2 (Continued)

GENERAL JOURNAL

PAGE 7

	DATE	DESCRIPTION	POST. REF.	DEBIT	CREDIT	
1						1
2						2
3						3
4						4
5						5
6						6
7						7
8						8
9						9
10						10
11						11
12						12
13						13
14						14
15						15
16						16
17						17
18						18
19						19
20						20
21						21
22						22
23						23
24						24
25						25
26						26
27						27
28						28
29						29
30						30
31						31
32						32
33						33
34						34

Comprehensive Problem 1, Period 2 (Continued)

2., 6., and 11.

GENERAL LEDGER

ACCOUNT Cash ACCOUNT NO. 101

DATE		ITEM	POST. REF.	DEBIT	CREDIT	BALANCE DEBIT	BALANCE CREDIT
20-- Apr.	30	Balance	✓			130,650.00	

ACCOUNT Accounts Receivable ACCOUNT NO. 122

DATE		ITEM	POST. REF.	DEBIT	CREDIT	BALANCE DEBIT	BALANCE CREDIT

Comprehensive Problem 1, Period 2 (Continued)

ACCOUNT Office Supplies ACCOUNT NO. 142

DATE		ITEM	POST. REF.	DEBIT	CREDIT	BALANCE DEBIT	BALANCE CREDIT
20-- Apr.	30	Balance	✓			100 00	

ACCOUNT Food Supplies ACCOUNT NO. 144

DATE		ITEM	POST. REF.	DEBIT	CREDIT	BALANCE DEBIT	BALANCE CREDIT
20-- Apr.	30	Balance	✓			8000 00	

ACCOUNT Prepaid Insurance ACCOUNT NO. 145

DATE		ITEM	POST. REF.	DEBIT	CREDIT	BALANCE DEBIT	BALANCE CREDIT
20-- Apr.	30	Balance	✓			7500 00	

ACCOUNT Prepaid Subscriptions ACCOUNT NO. 146

DATE		ITEM	POST. REF.	DEBIT	CREDIT	BALANCE DEBIT	BALANCE CREDIT

Comprehensive Problem 1, Period 2 (Continued)

ACCOUNT Land ACCOUNT NO. 161

DATE		ITEM	POST. REF.	DEBIT	CREDIT	BALANCE DEBIT	BALANCE CREDIT

ACCOUNT Buildings ACCOUNT NO. 171

DATE		ITEM	POST. REF.	DEBIT	CREDIT	BALANCE DEBIT	BALANCE CREDIT

ACCOUNT Accumulated Depreciation—Buildings ACCOUNT NO. 171.1

DATE		ITEM	POST. REF.	DEBIT	CREDIT	BALANCE DEBIT	BALANCE CREDIT

ACCOUNT Fishing Boats ACCOUNT NO. 181

DATE		ITEM	POST. REF.	DEBIT	CREDIT	BALANCE DEBIT	BALANCE CREDIT
20-- Apr.	30	Balance	✓			60,000.00	

Comprehensive Problem 1, Period 2 (Continued)

ACCOUNT Accumulated Depreciation—Fishing Boats ACCOUNT NO. 181.1

DATE		ITEM	POST. REF.	DEBIT	CREDIT	BALANCE DEBIT	BALANCE CREDIT
20-- Apr.	30	Balance	✓				1,000 00

ACCOUNT Surround Sound System ACCOUNT NO. 182

DATE		ITEM	POST. REF.	DEBIT	CREDIT	BALANCE DEBIT	BALANCE CREDIT

ACCOUNT Accumulated Depreciation—Surround Sound System ACCOUNT NO. 182.1

DATE		ITEM	POST. REF.	DEBIT	CREDIT	BALANCE DEBIT	BALANCE CREDIT

ACCOUNT Big Screen TV ACCOUNT NO. 183

DATE		ITEM	POST. REF.	DEBIT	CREDIT	BALANCE DEBIT	BALANCE CREDIT

ACCOUNT Accumulated Depreciation—Big Screen TV ACCOUNT NO. 183.1

DATE		ITEM	POST. REF.	DEBIT	CREDIT	BALANCE DEBIT	BALANCE CREDIT

Comprehensive Problem 1, Period 2 (Continued)

ACCOUNT Accounts Payable ACCOUNT NO. 202

DATE		ITEM	POST. REF.	DEBIT	CREDIT	BALANCE DEBIT	BALANCE CREDIT
20-- Apr.	30	Balance	✓				66,500.00

ACCOUNT Wages Payable ACCOUNT NO. 219

DATE		ITEM	POST. REF.	DEBIT	CREDIT	BALANCE DEBIT	BALANCE CREDIT
20-- Apr.	30	Balance	✓				500.00

ACCOUNT Bob Night, Capital ACCOUNT NO. 311

DATE		ITEM	POST. REF.	DEBIT	CREDIT	BALANCE DEBIT	BALANCE CREDIT
20-- Apr.	30	Balance	✓				138,250.00

ACCOUNT Bob Night, Drawing ACCOUNT NO. 312

DATE		ITEM	POST. REF.	DEBIT	CREDIT	BALANCE DEBIT	BALANCE CREDIT

Name ______________________________

Comprehensive Problem 1, Period 2 (Continued)

ACCOUNT Income Summary ACCOUNT NO. 313

DATE	ITEM	POST. REF.	DEBIT	CREDIT	BALANCE DEBIT	BALANCE CREDIT

ACCOUNT Registration Fees ACCOUNT NO. 401

DATE	ITEM	POST. REF.	DEBIT	CREDIT	BALANCE DEBIT	BALANCE CREDIT

ACCOUNT Vending Commission Revenue ACCOUNT NO. 404

DATE	ITEM	POST. REF.	DEBIT	CREDIT	BALANCE DEBIT	BALANCE CREDIT

ACCOUNT Wages Expense ACCOUNT NO. 511

DATE	ITEM	POST. REF.	DEBIT	CREDIT	BALANCE DEBIT	BALANCE CREDIT

Comprehensive Problem 1, Period 2 (Continued)

ACCOUNT Advertising Expense ACCOUNT NO. 512

DATE		ITEM	POST. REF.	DEBIT	CREDIT	BALANCE DEBIT	BALANCE CREDIT

ACCOUNT Rent Expense ACCOUNT NO. 521

DATE		ITEM	POST. REF.	DEBIT	CREDIT	BALANCE DEBIT	BALANCE CREDIT

ACCOUNT Office Supplies Expense ACCOUNT NO. 523

DATE		ITEM	POST. REF.	DEBIT	CREDIT	BALANCE DEBIT	BALANCE CREDIT

ACCOUNT Food Supplies Expense ACCOUNT NO. 524

DATE		ITEM	POST. REF.	DEBIT	CREDIT	BALANCE DEBIT	BALANCE CREDIT

Comprehensive Problem 1, Period 2 (Continued)

ACCOUNT Telephone Expense ACCOUNT NO. 525

DATE	ITEM	POST. REF.	DEBIT	CREDIT	BALANCE DEBIT	BALANCE CREDIT

ACCOUNT Utilities Expense ACCOUNT NO. 533

DATE	ITEM	POST. REF.	DEBIT	CREDIT	BALANCE DEBIT	BALANCE CREDIT

ACCOUNT Insurance Expense ACCOUNT NO. 535

DATE	ITEM	POST. REF.	DEBIT	CREDIT	BALANCE DEBIT	BALANCE CREDIT

ACCOUNT Postage Expense ACCOUNT NO. 536

DATE	ITEM	POST. REF.	DEBIT	CREDIT	BALANCE DEBIT	BALANCE CREDIT

Comprehensive Problem 1, Period 2 (Continued)

ACCOUNT Repair Expense ACCOUNT NO. 537

DATE		ITEM	POST. REF.	DEBIT	CREDIT	BALANCE DEBIT	BALANCE CREDIT

ACCOUNT Depreciation Expense—Buildings ACCOUNT NO. 540

DATE		ITEM	POST. REF.	DEBIT	CREDIT	BALANCE DEBIT	BALANCE CREDIT

ACCOUNT Depreciation Expense—Surround Sound System ACCOUNT NO. 541

DATE		ITEM	POST. REF.	DEBIT	CREDIT	BALANCE DEBIT	BALANCE CREDIT

ACCOUNT Depreciation Expense—Fishing Boats ACCOUNT NO. 542

DATE		ITEM	POST. REF.	DEBIT	CREDIT	BALANCE DEBIT	BALANCE CREDIT

Comprehensive Problem 1, Period 2 (Continued)

ACCOUNT Depreciation Expense—Big Screen TV ACCOUNT NO. 543

DATE		ITEM	POST. REF.	DEBIT	CREDIT	BALANCE DEBIT	BALANCE CREDIT

ACCOUNT Satellite Programming Expense ACCOUNT NO. 546

DATE		ITEM	POST. REF.	DEBIT	CREDIT	BALANCE DEBIT	BALANCE CREDIT

ACCOUNT Subscriptions Expense ACCOUNT NO. 548

DATE		ITEM	POST. REF.	DEBIT	CREDIT	BALANCE DEBIT	BALANCE CREDIT

Comprehensive Problem 1, Period 2 (Continued)
3. and 4.

	ACCOUNT TITLE	TRIAL BALANCE		ADJUSTMENTS	
		DEBIT	CREDIT	DEBIT	CREDIT
1					
2					
3					
4					
5					
6					
7					
8					
9					
10					
11					
12					
13					
14					
15					
16					
17					
18					
19					
20					
21					
22					
23					
24					
25					
26					
27					
28					
29					
30					
31					
32					
33					
34					
35					
36					
37					
38					
39					
40					

Name ______________________________

Comprehensive Problem 1, Period 2 (Continued)

ADJUSTED TRIAL BALANCE		INCOME STATEMENT		BALANCE SHEET		
DEBIT	CREDIT	DEBIT	CREDIT	DEBIT	CREDIT	
						1
						2
						3
						4
						5
						6
						7
						8
						9
						10
						11
						12
						13
						14
						15
						16
						17
						18
						19
						20
						21
						22
						23
						24
						25
						26
						27
						28
						29
						30
						31
						32
						33
						34
						35
						36
						37
						38
						39
						40

Comprehensive Problem 1, Period 2 (Continued)

5.

GENERAL JOURNAL

PAGE 8

	DATE		DESCRIPTION	POST. REF.	DEBIT	CREDIT	
1							1
2							2
3							3
4							4
5							5
6							6
7							7
8							8
9							9
10							10
11							11
12							12
13							13
14							14
15							15
16							16
17							17
18							18
19							19
20							20
21							21
22							22
23							23
24							24
25							25
26							26
27							27
28							28
29							29
30							30
31							31
32							32
33							33
34							34
35							35

Comprehensive Problem 1, Period 2 (Continued)

7.

8.

Comprehensive Problem 1, Period 2 (Continued)

9.

Comprehensive Problem 1, Period 2 (Continued)

10.

GENERAL JOURNAL

PAGE 9

	DATE		DESCRIPTION	POST. REF.	DEBIT	CREDIT	
1							1
2							2
3							3
4							4
5							5
6							6
7							7
8							8
9							9
10							10
11							11
12							12
13							13
14							14
15							15
16							16
17							17
18							18
19							19
20							20
21							21
22							22
23							23
24							24
25							25
26							26
27							27
28							28
29							29
30							30
31							31
32							32
33							33
34							34
35							35

Comprehensive Problem 1, Period 2 (Concluded)

12.

ACCOUNT TITLE	ACCT. NO.	DEBIT BALANCE	CREDIT BALANCE

Name ______________________________

Exercise 7-1A

1. ____________________
2. ____________________
3. ____________________
4. ____________________
5. ____________________
6. ____________________
7. ____________________

Exercise 7-2A

DEPOSIT TICKET 63-1209/631

WIZARD BANK
3711 Buena Vista Dr.
Orlando, FL 32811-1314

Date________________________ 20____

CHECKS AND OTHER ITEMS ARE RECEIVED FOR DEPOSIT SUBJECT TO THE TERMS AND CONDITIONS OF THIS FINANCIAL INSTITUTION'S ACCOUNT AGREEMENT.

____
SIGN HERE ONLY IF CASH RECEIVED FROM DEPOSIT

⑆063112094⑆ 0001632475⑈

CURRENCY			
COIN			
CHECKS			
TOTAL FROM OTHER SIDE			
SUBTOTAL			
LESS CASH RECEIVED			
NET DEPOSIT			

Exercise 7-3A

No. 1

DATE ____________ 20____
TO ____________________
FOR ____________________

ACCT. ____________________

	DOLLARS	CENTS
BAL BRO'T FOR'D		
AMT. DEPOSITED		
TOTAL		
AMT. THIS CHECK		
BAL CAR'D FOR'D		

No. 1 63-1209/631

____________________ 20______

PAY TO THE ORDER OF ____ $ ____________

____ Dollars

WIZARD BANK
3711 Buena Vista Dr.
Orlando, FL 32811-1314

FOR CLASSROOM USE ONLY

MEMO____________________ BY ____________________

⑆063112094⑆ 0001632475⑈

Exercise 7-4A

	Ending Bank Balance	Ending Checkbook Balance
1.		
2.		
3.		
4.		
5.		
6.		
7.		

Exercise 7-5A

GENERAL JOURNAL PAGE

	DATE		DESCRIPTION	POST. REF.	DEBIT	CREDIT	
1							1
2							2
3							3
4							4
5							5
6							6
7							7
8							8
9							9
10							10
11							11
12							12
13							13
14							14
15							15
16							16
17							17
18							18
19							19
20							20
21							21

Name ______________________________

Exercise 7-6A

GENERAL JOURNAL

PAGE

DATE		DESCRIPTION	POST. REF.	DEBIT	CREDIT

Exercise 7-7A

GENERAL JOURNAL

PAGE

	DATE		DESCRIPTION	POST. REF.	DEBIT	CREDIT	
1							1
2							2
3							3
4							4
5							5
6							6
7							7
8							8
9							9
10							10
11							11
12							12
13							13
14							14
15							15
16							16
17							17
18							18
19							19
20							20
21							21
22							22
23							23
24							24
25							25
26							26
27							27
28							28
29							29
30							30
31							31
32							32
33							33
34							34
35							35
36							36

Name ______________________________

Problem 7-8A

1.

Problem 7-8A (Concluded)

2.

GENERAL JOURNAL

PAGE

	DATE		DESCRIPTION	POST. REF.	DEBIT	CREDIT	
1							1
2							2
3							3
4							4
5							5
6							6
7							7
8							8
9							9
10							10
11							11
12							12
13							13
14							14
15							15

Name ________________________________

Problem 7-9A

1.

Problem 7-9A (Concluded)

2.

GENERAL JOURNAL

PAGE

	DATE	DESCRIPTION	POST. REF.	DEBIT	CREDIT	
1						1
2						2
3						3
4						4
5						5
6						6
7						7
8						8
9						9
10						10
11						11
12						12
13						13
14						14
15						15
16						16
17						17
18						18
19						19

Name ______________________________

Problem 7-10A

1. and 3.

GENERAL JOURNAL

PAGE

	DATE		DESCRIPTION	POST. REF.	DEBIT	CREDIT	
1							1
2							2
3							3
4							4
5							5
6							6
7							7
8							8
9							9
10							10
11							11
12							12
13							13

Problem 7-10A (Concluded)

2. and 3.

PETTY CASH PAYMENTS FOR MONTH OF 20-- PAGE

					DISTRIBUTION OF PAYMENTS								
	DAY	DESCRIPTION	VOU. NO.	TOTAL AMOUNT	OFFICE SUPPLIES	POSTAGE EXPENSE	CHARIT. CONTRIB. EXPENSE	TELEPHONE EXPENSE	TRAVEL & ENTER. EXPENSE	MISC. EXPENSE	ACCOUNT	AMOUNT	
1													1
2													2
3													3
4													4
5													5
6													6
7													7
8													8
9													9
10													10
11													11
12													12
13													13
14													14
15													15
16													16
17													17
18													18
19													19
20													20
21													21
22													22

Problem 7-11A

1.

GENERAL JOURNAL

PAGE 8

	DATE	DESCRIPTION	POST. REF.	DEBIT	CREDIT	
1						1
2						2
3						3
4						4
5						5
6						6
7						7
8						8
9						9
10						10
11						11
12						12
13						13
14						14
15						15
16						16
17						17
18						18
19						19
20						20
21						21
22						22
23						23

2.

ACCOUNT ______________________________ ACCOUNT NO. ________

DATE	ITEM	POST. REF.	DEBIT	CREDIT	BALANCE	
					DEBIT	CREDIT

3. The balance represents:

____

Exercise 7-1B

1. ____________________
2. ____________________
3. ____________________
4. ____________________
5. ____________________
6. ____________________
7. ____________________

Exercise 7-2B

63-1209
631

DEPOSIT TICKET

WIZARD BANK
3711 Buena Vista Dr.
Orlando, FL 32811-1314

Date ____________________ 20____

CHECKS AND OTHER ITEMS ARE RECEIVED FOR DEPOSIT SUBJECT TO THE TERMS AND CONDITIONS OF THIS FINANCIAL INSTITUTION'S ACCOUNT AGREEMENT.

____
SIGN HERE ONLY IF CASH RECEIVED FROM DEPOSIT

⑆063112094⑆ 0001632475⑈

CURRENCY			
COIN			
CHECKS			
TOTAL FROM OTHER SIDE			
SUBTOTAL			
LESS CASH RECEIVED			
NET DEPOSIT			

Exercise 7-3B

No. 1

DATE ____________ 20____
TO ____________________
FOR ____________________

ACCT. ____________________

	DOLLARS	CENTS
BAL BRO'T FOR'D		
AMT. DEPOSITED		
TOTAL		
AMT. THIS CHECK		
BAL CAR'D FOR'D		

No. 1 63-1209/631

____________________ 20________

PAY TO THE ORDER OF ____ $ ____________

____ Dollars

WIZARD BANK
3711 Buena Vista Dr.
Orlando, FL 32811-1314

FOR CLASSROOM USE ONLY

MEMO ____________________ BY ____________________

⑆063112094⑆ 0001632475⑈

Name ________________________________

Exercise 7-4B

	Ending Bank Balance	Ending Checkbook Balance
1.		
2.		
3.		
4.		
5.		
6.		
7.		

Exercise 7-5B

GENERAL JOURNAL

PAGE

	DATE		DESCRIPTION	POST. REF.	DEBIT	CREDIT	
1							1
2							2
3							3
4							4
5							5
6							6
7							7
8							8
9							9
10							10
11							11
12							12
13							13
14							14
15							15
16							16
17							17
18							18
19							19
20							20
21							21

Exercise 7-6B

GENERAL JOURNAL

PAGE

DATE		DESCRIPTION	POST. REF.	DEBIT	CREDIT

Exercise 7-7B

GENERAL JOURNAL

PAGE

DATE		DESCRIPTION	POST. REF.	DEBIT	CREDIT

Problem 7-8B

1.

Problem 7-8B (Concluded)

2.

GENERAL JOURNAL

PAGE

	DATE		DESCRIPTION	POST. REF.	DEBIT	CREDIT	
1							1
2							2
3							3
4							4
5							5
6							6
7							7
8							8
9							9
10							10
11							11
12							12
13							13
14							14
15							15

Problem 7-9B

1.

Problem 7-9B (Concluded)

2.

GENERAL JOURNAL

PAGE

	DATE		DESCRIPTION	POST. REF.	DEBIT	CREDIT	
1							1
2							2
3							3
4							4
5							5
6							6
7							7
8							8
9							9
10							10
11							11
12							12
13							13
14							14
15							15
16							16
17							17
18							18
19							19

Problem 7-10B

1. and 3.

GENERAL JOURNAL

PAGE

	DATE		DESCRIPTION	POST. REF.	DEBIT	CREDIT	
1							1
2							2
3							3
4							4
5							5
6							6
7							7
8							8
9							9
10							10
11							11
12							12
13							13

Problem 7-10B (Concluded)

2. and 3.

PETTY CASH PAYMENTS FOR MONTH OF 20-- PAGE

					DISTRIBUTION OF PAYMENTS								
	DAY	DESCRIPTION	VOU. NO.	TOTAL AMOUNT	OFFICE SUPPLIES	POSTAGE EXPENSE	CHARIT. CONTRIB. EXPENSE	TELEPHONE EXPENSE	TRAVEL & ENTER. EXPENSE	MISC. EXPENSE	ACCOUNT	AMOUNT	
1													1
2													2
3													3
4													4
5													5
6													6
7													7
8													8
9													9
10													10
11													11
12													12
13													13
14													14
15													15
16													16
17													17
18													18
19													19
20													20
21													21
22													22

Problem 7-11B

1.

GENERAL JOURNAL

PAGE 8

	DATE		DESCRIPTION	POST. REF.	DEBIT	CREDIT	
1							1
2							2
3							3
4							4
5							5
6							6
7							7
8							8
9							9
10							10
11							11
12							12
13							13
14							14
15							15
16							16
17							17
18							18
19							19
20							20
21							21
22							22
23							23

2.

ACCOUNT ACCOUNT NO.

DATE		ITEM	POST. REF.	DEBIT	CREDIT	BALANCE	
						DEBIT	CREDIT

3. The balance represents:

Mastery Problem

1.

PETTY CASH PAYMENTS FOR MONTH OF 20-- PAGE

					DISTRIBUTION OF PAYMENTS								
	DAY	DESCRIPTION	VOU. NO.	TOTAL AMOUNT	TRUCK EXPENSE	POSTAGE EXPENSE	CHARIT. CONTRIB. EXPENSE	TELEPHONE EXPENSE	ADVERT. EXPENSE.	MISC. EXPENSE	ACCOUNT	AMOUNT	
1													1
2													2
3													3
4													4
5													5
6													6
7													7
8													8
9													9
10													10
11													11
12													12
13													13
14													14
15													15
16													16
17													17
18													18
19													19
20													20
21													21
22													22

Mastery Problem (Continued)
2. and 3.

GENERAL JOURNAL

PAGE 1

DATE	DESCRIPTION	POST. REF.	DEBIT	CREDIT

Mastery Problem (Concluded)

GENERAL JOURNAL

PAGE 2

	DATE		DESCRIPTION	POST. REF.	DEBIT	CREDIT	
1							1
2							2
3							3
4							4
5							5
6							6
7							7
8							8
9							9
10							10
11							11
12							12
13							13
14							14

3.

Challenge Problem

1. Panera Bakery

GENERAL JOURNAL PAGE

DATE		DESCRIPTION	POST. REF.	DEBIT	CREDIT

Name ______________________________

Challenge Problem (Concluded)

2. Lawrence Bank

GENERAL JOURNAL PAGE

DATE		DESCRIPTION	POST. REF.	DEBIT	CREDIT

APPENDIX: Internal Controls

Exercise 7Apx-1A

1. ____

____

2. ____

____

3. ____

____

4. ____

____

5. ____

____

Exercise 7Apx-2A

1. _____

2. _____

3. _____

4. _____

5. _____

Name ______________________________

Exercise 7Apx-3A

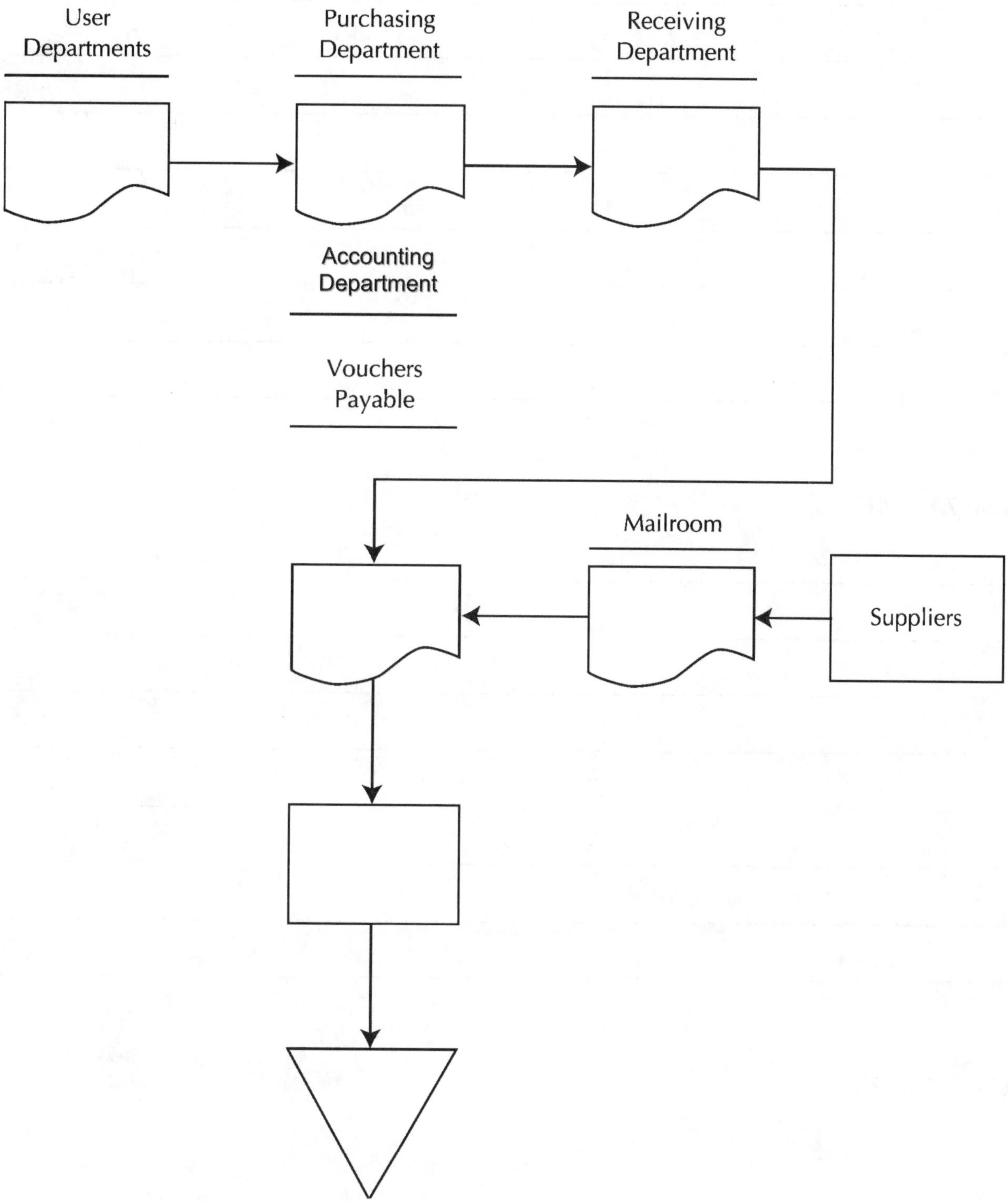

Problem 7Apx-4A

1. ______________________________

____

2. ______________________________

____

3. ______________________________

____

4. ______________________________

____

Exercise 7Apx-1B

1. ______________________________

____

2. ______________________________

____

3. ______________________________

____

4. ______________________________

____

Exercise 7Apx-2B

1. _____

2. _____

3. _____

4. _____

Name ______________________________

Exercise 7Apx-3B

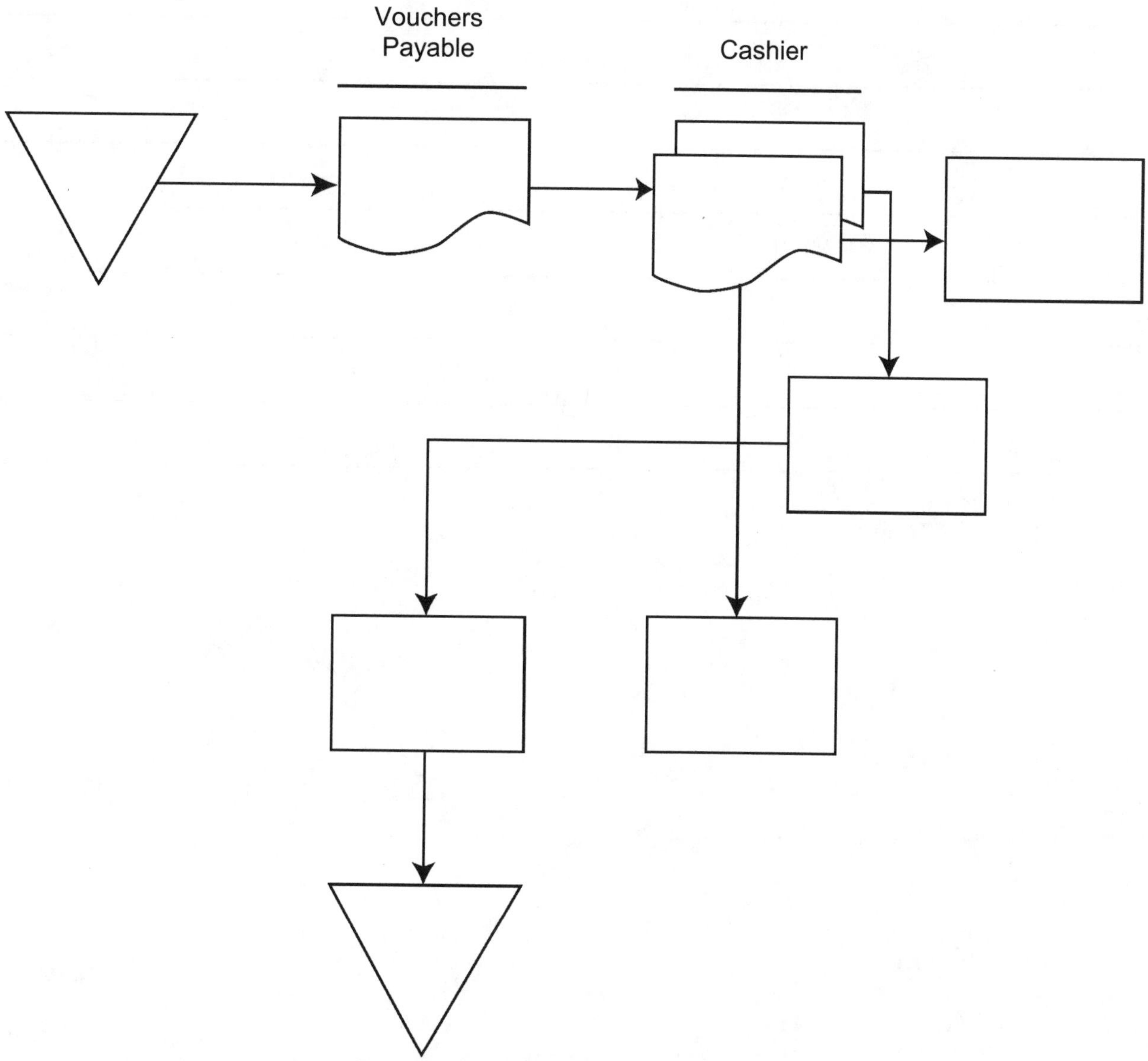

Problem 7Apx-4B

1. ______________________________

____

2. ______________________________

____

3. ______________________________

____

4. ______________________________

____

Name ______________________________

Exercise 8-1A

a. __________ regular hours × $10 per hour __________

b. __________ overtime hours × $15 per hour __________

c. Total gross wages __________

d. Federal income tax withholding
   (from tax tables in Figure 8-4) __________

e. Social Security withholding at 6.2% __________

f. Medicare withholding at 1.45% __________

g. Total withholding __________

h. Net pay __________

Exercise 8-2A

Exercise 8-3A

Exercise 8-4A

	Marital Status	Total Weekly Earnings	Number of Allowances	Amount of Withholding
a.	S	$347.60	2	
b.	S	451.50	1	
c.	M	481.15	3	
d.	S	490.52	0	
e.	M	701.89	5	

Exercise 8-5A

Cumul. Pay Before Current Weekly Payroll	Current Gross Pay	Year-to-Date Earnings	Soc. Sec. Maximum	Amount Over Max. Soc. Sec.	Amount Subject to Soc. Sec.	Soc. Sec. Tax Withheld	Medicare Tax Withheld
$ 22,000	$1,700		$110,100				
54,000	4,200		110,100				
107,500	3,925		110,100				
109,500	4,600		110,100				

Exercise 8-6A

GENERAL JOURNAL PAGE

	DATE		DESCRIPTION	POST. REF.	DEBIT	CREDIT	
1							1
2							2
3							3
4							4
5							5
6							6
7							7
8							8
9							9

Exercise 8-7A

GENERAL JOURNAL PAGE

	DATE		DESCRIPTION	POST. REF.	DEBIT	CREDIT	
1							1
2							2
3							3
4							4
5							5
6							6
7							7
8							8
9							9

Name ______________________________

Problem 8-8A

1.

2.

GENERAL JOURNAL

PAGE

	DATE		DESCRIPTION	POST. REF.	DEBIT	CREDIT	
1							1
2							2
3							3
4							4
5							5
6							6
7							7
8							8
9							9
10							10
11							11
12							12
13							13
14							14
15							15

Problem 8-9A

1.

PAYROLL REGISTER

				EARNINGS				TAXABLE EARNINGS	
	NAME	NO. ALLOW.	MARIT. STATUS	REGULAR	OVERTIME	TOTAL	CUMULATIVE TOTAL	UNEMPLOY. COMP.	SOCIAL SECURITY
1									
2									
3									
4									
5									
6									
7									
8									
9									
10									
11									
12									
13									
14									

Name ______________________________

Problem 8-9A (Concluded)

FOR PERIOD ENDED 20--

DEDUCTIONS									
FEDERAL INCOME TAX	SOCIAL SECURITY TAX	MEDICARE TAX	CITY TAX	HEALTH INSUR.	OTHER	TOTAL	NET PAY	CK. NO.	
									1
									2
									3
									4
									5
									6
									7
									8
									9
									10
									11
									12
									13
									14

2.

GENERAL JOURNAL

PAGE

	DATE	DESCRIPTION	POST. REF.	DEBIT	CREDIT	
1						1
2						2
3						3
4						4
5						5
6						6
7						7
8						8
9						9
10						10
11						11
12						12
13						13
14						14

Problem 8-10A

EMPLOYEE EARNINGS RECORD

20 -- PERIOD ENDED	EARNINGS				TAXABLE EARNINGS		DEDUCTIONS	
	REGULAR	OVERTIME	TOTAL	CUMULATIVE TOTAL	UNEMPLOY. COMP.	SOCIAL SECURITY	FEDERAL INCOME TAX	SOCIAL SECURITY TAX

GENDER		DEPARTMENT	OCCUPATION	SOCIAL SECURITY NO.	MARITAL STATUS	ALLOW-ANCES
M	F					

Name ______________________________

Problem 8-10A (Concluded)

FOR PERIOD ENDED 20--

DEDUCTIONS						
MEDICARE TAX	CITY TAX	HEALTH INSURANCE	OTHER	TOTAL	CK. NO.	AMOUNT

PAY RATE	DATE OF BIRTH	DATE HIRED	NAME/ADDRESS	EMP. NO.

Exercise 8-1B

a. __________ regular hours × $12 per hour __________

b. __________ overtime hours × $18 per hour __________

c. Total gross wages __________

d. Federal income tax withholding
(from tax tables in Figure 8-4) __________

e. Social Security withholding at 6.2% __________

f. Medicare withholding at 1.45% __________

g. Total withholding __________

h. Net pay __________

Exercise 8-2B

____

____

____

____

Exercise 8-3B

____

____

____

____

____

____

____

____

Exercise 8-4B

	Marital Status	Total Weekly Earnings	Number of Allowances	Amount of Withholding
a.	M	$546.00	4	__________
b.	M	390.00	3	__________
c.	S	461.39	2	__________
d.	M	522.88	2	__________
e.	S	612.00	0	__________

Exercise 8-5B

Cumul. Pay Before Current Weekly Payroll	Current Gross Pay	Year-to-Date Earnings	Soc. Sec. Maximum	Amount Over Max. Soc. Sec.	Amount Subject to Soc. Sec.	Soc. Sec. Tax Withheld	Medicare Tax Withheld
$ 31,000	$1,500		$110,100				
53,000	2,860		110,100				
107,200	3,140		110,100				
109,500	2,920		110,100				

Exercise 8-6B

GENERAL JOURNAL PAGE

	DATE		DESCRIPTION	POST. REF.	DEBIT	CREDIT	
1							1
2							2
3							3
4							4
5							5
6							6
7							7
8							8
9							9
10							10
11							11
12							12
13							13
14							14
15							15
16							16
17							17
18							18
19							19
20							20
21							21
22							22

Exercise 8-7B

GENERAL JOURNAL PAGE

	DATE		DESCRIPTION	POST. REF.	DEBIT	CREDIT	
1							1
2							2
3							3
4							4
5							5
6							6
7							7
8							8
9							9
10							10
11							11
12							12
13							13

Problem 8-8B

1.

Problem 8-8B (Concluded)

2.

GENERAL JOURNAL

PAGE

DATE		DESCRIPTION	POST. REF.	DEBIT	CREDIT

Problem 8-9B

1.

PAYROLL REGISTER

	NAME	NO. ALLOW.	MARIT. STATUS	EARNINGS				TAXABLE EARNINGS	
				REGULAR	OVERTIME	TOTAL	CUMULATIVE TOTAL	UNEMPLOY. COMP.	SOCIAL SECURITY
1									
2									
3									
4									
5									
6									
7									
8									
9									
10									
11									
12									
13									
14									

Problem 8-9B (Concluded)

FOR PERIOD ENDED 20--

DEDUCTIONS									
FEDERAL INCOME TAX	SOCIAL SECURITY TAX	MEDICARE TAX	CITY TAX	HEALTH INSUR.	OTHER	TOTAL	NET PAY	CK. NO.	
									1
									2
									3
									4
									5
									6
									7
									8
									9
									10
									11
									12
									13
									14

2.

GENERAL JOURNAL

PAGE

	DATE	DESCRIPTION	POST. REF.	DEBIT	CREDIT	
1						1
2						2
3						3
4						4
5						5
6						6
7						7
8						8
9						9
10						10
11						11
12						12
13						13
14						14

Problem 8-10B

EMPLOYEE EARNINGS RECORD

20 -- PERIOD ENDED	EARNINGS: REGULAR	EARNINGS: OVERTIME	EARNINGS: TOTAL	EARNINGS: CUMULATIVE TOTAL	TAXABLE EARNINGS: UNEMPLOY. COMP.	TAXABLE EARNINGS: SOCIAL SECURITY	DEDUCTIONS: FEDERAL INCOME TAX	DEDUCTIONS: SOCIAL SECURITY TAX

GENDER	DEPARTMENT	OCCUPATION	SOCIAL SECURITY NO.	MARITAL STATUS	ALLOW-ANCES
M / F					

Name ______________________________

Problem 8-10B (Concluded)

FOR PERIOD ENDED 20--

DEDUCTIONS							
MEDICARE TAX	CITY TAX	HEALTH INSURANCE	OTHER		TOTAL	CK. NO.	AMOUNT

PAY RATE	DATE OF BIRTH	DATE HIRED	NAME/ADDRESS	EMP. NO.

Mastery Problem

1.

PAYROLL REGISTER

				EARNINGS				TAXABLE EARNINGS	
	NAME	NO. ALLOW.	MARIT. STATUS	REGULAR	OVERTIME	TOTAL	CUMULATIVE TOTAL	UNEMPLOY. COMP.	SOCIAL SECURITY
1									
2									
3									
4									
5									
6									
7									
8									
9									
10									
11									
12									
13									
14									

3.

EMPLOYEE EARNINGS RECORD

	EARNINGS				TAXABLE EARNINGS		
20 -- PERIOD ENDED	REGULAR	OVERTIME	TOTAL	CUMULATIVE TOTAL	UNEMPLOY. COMP.	SOCIAL SECURITY	FEDERAL INCOME TAX
11/4	330 00	33 00	363 00	6,145 50	363 00	363 00	6 00
11/11	440 00	49 50	489 50	6,635 00	489 50	489 50	18 00
11/18							
11/25							

GENDER		DEPARTMENT	OCCUPATION	SOCIAL SECURITY NO.	MARITAL STATUS
M	F				

Mastery Problem (Continued)

FOR PERIOD ENDED 20--

DEDUCTIONS																
FEDERAL INCOME TAX		SOCIAL SECURITY TAX		MEDICARE TAX		STATE INCOME TAX		HEALTH INSURANCE		CREDIT UNION		TOTAL		NET PAY		CK. NO.
																1
																2
																3
																4
																5
																6
																7
																8
																9
																10
																11
																12
																13
																14

FOR PERIOD ENDED 20--

DEDUCTIONS												NET PAY		
SOCIAL SECURITY TAX		MEDICARE TAX		STATE INCOME TAX		HEALTH INSURANCE		CREDIT UNION		TOTAL		CK. NO.	AMOUNT	
22	51	5	26	12	71			72	60	119	08	121	243	92
30	35	7	10	17	13			97	90	170	48	229	319	02

ALLOWANCES	PAY RATE	DATE OF BIRTH	DATE HIRED	NAME/ADDRESS	EMP. NO.

Mastery Problem (Concluded)

2.

GENERAL JOURNAL

PAGE

DATE		DESCRIPTION	POST. REF.	DEBIT	CREDIT

Name ____________________

Challenge Problem

1.

GENERAL JOURNAL

PAGE

	DATE		DESCRIPTION	POST. REF.	DEBIT	CREDIT	
1							1
2							2
3							3
4							4
5							5
6							6
7							7
8							8
9							9
10							10

2.

Exercise 9-1A

GENERAL JOURNAL

PAGE

	DATE		DESCRIPTION	POST. REF.	DEBIT	CREDIT	
1							1
2							2
3							3
4							4
5							5
6							6
7							7

Exercise 9-2A

GENERAL JOURNAL

PAGE

	DATE		DESCRIPTION	POST. REF.	DEBIT	CREDIT	
1							1
2							2
3							3
4							4
5							5
6							6
7							7

Exercise 9-3A

Name	Current Earnings	Taxable Earnings: Unemploy. Comp.	Taxable Earnings: Social Security
Jordahl			
Keesling			
Palmer			
Soltis			
Stout			
Xia			
Total			

GENERAL JOURNAL PAGE

	DATE		DESCRIPTION	POST. REF.	DEBIT	CREDIT	
1							1
2							2
3							3
4							4
5							5
6							6
7							7

Exercise 9-4A

Exercise 9-5A

GENERAL JOURNAL PAGE

	DATE		DESCRIPTION	POST. REF.	DEBIT	CREDIT	
1							1
2							2
3							3
4							4
5							5
6							6
7							7
8							8
9							9
10							10
11							11
12							12

Exercise 9-6A

1.

GENERAL JOURNAL PAGE

	DATE		DESCRIPTION	POST. REF.	DEBIT	CREDIT	
1							1
2							2
3							3
4							4
5							5

2.

GENERAL JOURNAL PAGE

	DATE		DESCRIPTION	POST. REF.	DEBIT	CREDIT	
1							1
2							2
3							3
4							4

Problem 9-7A

1.

		Taxable Earnings	
Name	**Current Earnings**	**Unemploy. Comp.**	**Social Security**
Click, Katelyn			
Coombs, Michelle			
Faus, Erin			
Lenihan, Marcus			
McMahon, Drew			
Newell, Marg			
Stevens, Matt			
Total			

2.

GENERAL JOURNAL

PAGE

	DATE		DESCRIPTION	POST. REF.	DEBIT	CREDIT	
1							1
2							2
3							3
4							4
5							5
6							6
7							7
8							8
9							9
10							10

Name ______________________________

Problem 9-8A

1.

GENERAL JOURNAL

PAGE

DATE		DESCRIPTION	POST. REF.	DEBIT	CREDIT

Problem 9-8A (Continued)

GENERAL JOURNAL

PAGE

DATE		DESCRIPTION	POST. REF.	DEBIT	CREDIT

Problem 9-8A (Concluded)

2.

Cash 101

Employee Federal Income Tax Payable 211

Social Security Tax Payable 212

Medicare Tax Payable 213

Savings Bond Deductions Payable 218

FUTA Tax Payable 221

SUTA Tax Payable 222

Wages and Salaries Expense 511

Payroll Taxes Expense 530

Problem 9-9A

1.

GENERAL JOURNAL

PAGE

	DATE		DESCRIPTION	POST. REF.	DEBIT	CREDIT	
1							1
2							2
3							3
4							4
5							5
6							6

2.

GENERAL JOURNAL

PAGE

	DATE		DESCRIPTION	POST. REF.	DEBIT	CREDIT	
1							1
2							2
3							3
4							4
5							5
6							6

Problem 9-9A (Concluded)

3.

GENERAL JOURNAL

PAGE

	DATE		DESCRIPTION	POST. REF.	DEBIT	CREDIT	
1							1
2							2
3							3
4							4
5							5

Exercise 9-1B

GENERAL JOURNAL

PAGE

	DATE		DESCRIPTION	POST. REF.	DEBIT	CREDIT	
1							1
2							2
3							3
4							4
5							5
6							6
7							7
8							8
9							9

Exercise 9-2B

GENERAL JOURNAL

PAGE

	DATE		DESCRIPTION	POST. REF.	DEBIT	CREDIT	
1							1
2							2
3							3
4							4
5							5
6							6
7							7
8							8

Exercise 9-3B

		Taxable Earnings	
Name	**Current Earnings**	**Unemploy. Comp.**	**Social Security**
Carlson			
Delgado			
Lewis			
Nixon			
Shippe			
Watts			
Total			

Name ______________________________

Exercise 9-3B (Concluded)

GENERAL JOURNAL

PAGE

	DATE		DESCRIPTION	POST. REF.	DEBIT	CREDIT	
1							1
2							2
3							3
4							4
5							5
6							6
7							7

Exercise 9-4B: See page WP-302.

Exercise 9-5B

GENERAL JOURNAL

PAGE

	DATE		DESCRIPTION	POST. REF.	DEBIT	CREDIT	
1							1
2							2
3							3
4							4
5							5
6							6
7							7
8							8
9							9
10							10
11							11
12							12
13							13
14							14

Exercise 9-4B

Exercise 9-6B

1.

GENERAL JOURNAL PAGE

	DATE		DESCRIPTION	POST. REF.	DEBIT	CREDIT	
1							1
2							2
3							3
4							4
5							5

2.

GENERAL JOURNAL PAGE

	DATE		DESCRIPTION	POST. REF.	DEBIT	CREDIT	
1							1
2							2
3							3
4							4
5							5

Name ______________________

Problem 9-7B

1.

Name	Current Earnings	Taxable Earnings: Unemploy. Comp.	Taxable Earnings: Social Security
Ackers, Alice			
Conley, Dorothy			
Davis, James			
Lawrence, Kevin			
Rawlings, Judy			
Tanaka, Sumio			
Vadillo, Raynette			
Total			

2.

GENERAL JOURNAL

PAGE

	DATE		DESCRIPTION	POST. REF.	DEBIT	CREDIT	
1							1
2							2
3							3
4							4
5							5
6							6
7							7
8							8
9							9
10							10
11							11
12							12

Problem 9-8B

1.

GENERAL JOURNAL

PAGE

DATE		DESCRIPTION	POST. REF.	DEBIT	CREDIT

Name ______________________________

Problem 9-8B (Continued)

GENERAL JOURNAL

PAGE

	DATE		DESCRIPTION	POST. REF.	DEBIT	CREDIT	
1							1
2							2
3							3
4							4
5							5
6							6
7							7
8							8
9							9
10							10
11							11
12							12
13							13
14							14
15							15
16							16
17							17
18							18
19							19
20							20
21							21
22							22
23							23
24							24
25							25
26							26
27							27
28							28
29							29
30							30
31							31
32							32
33							33
34							34
35							35

Problem 9-8B (Concluded)

2.

Cash	101

Employee Federal Income Tax Payable	211

Social Security Tax Payable	212

Medicare Tax Payable	213

Savings Bond Deductions Payable	218

FUTA Tax Payable	221

SUTA Tax Payable	222

Wages and Salaries Expense	511

Payroll Taxes Expense	530

Name ______________________________

Problem 9-9B

1.

GENERAL JOURNAL PAGE

	DATE	DESCRIPTION	POST. REF.	DEBIT	CREDIT	
1						1
2						2
3						3
4						4
5						5
6						6

2.

GENERAL JOURNAL PAGE

	DATE	DESCRIPTION	POST. REF.	DEBIT	CREDIT	
1						1
2						2
3						3
4						4
5						5
6						6

Problem 9-9B (Concluded)

3.

GENERAL JOURNAL

PAGE

	DATE		DESCRIPTION	POST. REF.	DEBIT	CREDIT	
1							1
2							2
3							3
4							4

Name ______________________________

Mastery Problem

1., 2., and 3.

GENERAL JOURNAL

PAGE

	DATE		DESCRIPTION	POST. REF.	DEBIT	CREDIT	
1							1
2							2
3							3
4							4
5							5
6							6
7							7
8							8
9							9
10							10
11							11
12							12
13							13
14							14
15							15
16							16
17							17
18							18
19							19
20							20
21							21
22							22
23							23
24							24
25							25
26							26
27							27
28							28
29							29
30							30
31							31
32							32
33							33
34							34
35							35

Mastery Problem (Concluded)

GENERAL JOURNAL

PAGE

	DATE	DESCRIPTION	POST. REF.	DEBIT	CREDIT	
1						1
2						2
3						3
4						4
5						5
6						6
7						7
8						8
9						9
10						10
11						11
12						12
13						13
14						14
15						15
16						16
17						17
18						18
19						19
20						20
21						21
22						22
23						23
24						24
25						25
26						26
27						27
28						28
29						29
30						30
31						31
32						32
33						33
34						34
35						35

Challenge Problem

1.

2.

GENERAL JOURNAL PAGE

	DATE		DESCRIPTION	POST. REF.	DEBIT	CREDIT	
1							1
2							2
3							3
4							4
5							5
6							6
7							7

3.

NOTES

NOTES

Name ______________________________

Exercise 2-1A

Item	Account	Classification
Money in bank	Cash	____________
Office supplies	Supplies	____________
Money owed	Accounts Payable	____________
Office chairs	Office Furniture	____________
Net worth of owner	John Smith, Capital	____________
Money withdrawn by owner	John Smith, Drawing	____________
Money owed by customers	Accounts Receivable	____________

Exercise 2-2A

Assets	=	Liabilities	+	Owner's Equity
____________	=	$27,000	+	$17,000
$32,000	=	$18,000	+	____________
$27,000	=	____________	+	$20,000

Exercise 2-3A

	Assets	=	Liabilities	+	Owner's Equity
(a)	____________		____________		____________
Bal.	____________		____________		____________
(b)	____________		____________		____________
Bal.	____________		____________		____________
(c)	____________		____________		____________
	____________		____________		____________
Bal.	____________		____________		____________
(d)	____________		____________		____________
Bal.	____________		____________		____________

Exercise 2-4A

	Assets	=	Liabilities	+	Owner's Equity: Capital	−	Drawing	+	Revenues	−	Expenses	Description
Bal. from E 2-3A (d)												
(e)												
(f)												
(g)												
(h)												
(i)												
(j)												
(k)												
Bal.												

Exercise 2-5A

Account	Classification	Financial Statement
Cash		
Rent Expense		
Accounts Payable		
Service Fees		
Supplies		
Wages Expense		
Ramon Martinez, Drawing		
Ramon Martinez, Capital		
Prepaid Insurance		
Accounts Receivable		

Exercise 2-6A

Exercise 2-7A

Problem 2-8A

	Assets	=	Liabilities	+	Owner's Equity
1.					
2.					
3.					

Problem 2-9A: See page WP-7

Problem 2-10A

Problem 2-9A

	Assets				= Liabilities	+ Owner's Equity				
	(Items Owned)				(Amts. Owed)	(Owner's Investment)		(Earnings)		
	Cash	+ Accounts Receivable	+ Office Supplies	+ Prepaid Insurance	= Accounts Payable	+ J. Pembroke, Capital	– J. Pembroke, Drawing	+ Revenues	– Expenses	Description
(a)										
(b)										
(c)										
(d)										
(e)										
(f)										
(g)										
Bal.										

Problem 2-11A

Problem 2-12A

Exercise 2-1B

Account	Classification
Cash	________
Accounts Payable	________
Supplies	________
Bill Jones, Drawing	________
Prepaid Insurance	________
Accounts Receivable	________
Bill Jones, Capital	________

Exercise 2-2B

Assets	=	Liabilities	+	Owner's Equity
________	=	$20,000	+	$ 5,000
$30,000	=	$15,000	+	________
$20,000	=	________	+	$10,000

Exercise 2-3B

	Assets	=	Liabilities	+	Owner's Equity
(a)	________		________		________
Bal.	________		________		________
(b)	________		________		________
Bal.	________		________		________
(c)	________		________		________
	________		________		________
Bal.	________		________		________
(d)	________		________		________
Bal.	________		________		________

Exercise 2-4B

	Assets	=	Liabilities	+	Owner's Equity: Capital	–	Drawing	+	Revenues	–	Expenses	Description
Bal. from E 2-3B												
(d)												
(e)												
(f)												
(g)												
(h)												
(i)												
(j)												
(k)												
Bal.												

Name ______________________________

Exercise 2-5B

Account	Classification	Financial Statement
Cash		
Rent Expense		
Accounts Payable		
Service Fees		
Supplies		
Wages Expense		
Amanda Wong, Drawing		
Amanda Wong, Capital		
Prepaid Insurance		
Accounts Receivable		

Exercise 2-6B

Exercise 2-7B

Problem 2-8B

	Assets	=	Liabilities	+	Owner's Equity
1.					
2.					
3.					

Problem 2-9B: See page WP-13

Problem 2-10B

Name ____________________

Problem 2-9B

	Assets (Items Owned)				=	Liabilities (Amts. Owed)	+	Owner's Equity (Owner's Investment)			(Earnings)		Description
	Cash	+ Accounts Receivable	+ Office Supplies	+ Prepaid Insurance	=	Accounts Payable	+	D. Segal, Capital	−	D. Segal, Drawing	+ Revenues	− Expenses	Description
(a)													
(b)													
(c)													
(d)													
(e)													
(f)													
(g)													
Bal.													

Problem 2-11B

Problem 2-12B

Mastery Problem

1.

	Assets (Items Owned)						= Liabilities (Amts. Owed)	+ Owner's Equity (Owner's Investment)		(Earnings)		
	Cash	+ Accts. Rec.	+ Sup-plies	+ Prepaid Ins.	+ Tools	+ Van	= Accts. Payable	+ L. Vozniak, Capital	− L. Vozniak, Drawing	+ Rev.	− Exp.	Description
(a)												
(b)												
(c)												
(d)												
(e)												
(f)												
(g)												
(h)												
(i)												
(j)												
(k)												
(l)												
(m)												
(n)												
(o)												
(p)												
2. Bal.												

Mastery Problem (Continued)

3.

4.

Mastery Problem (Concluded)

5.

Challenge Problem

Cash from customers		
Cash paid for wages		
Cash paid for rent		
Cash paid for utilities		
Cash paid for insurance		
Cash paid for supplies		
Cash paid for telephone		
Total cash paid for operating items		
Difference between cash received from customers and		
cash paid for goods and services		

Name ______________________

Exercise 3-1A

Cash

500	100
400	200
600	

Exercise 3-2A

a. The cash account is increased with a .... ________
b. The owner's capital account is increased with a .... ________
c. The delivery equipment account is increased with a .... ________
d. The cash account is decreased with a .... ________
e. The liability account Accounts Payable is increased with a .... ________
f. The revenue account Delivery Fees is increased with a .... ________
g. The asset account Accounts Receivable is increased with a .... ________
h. The rent expense account is increased with a .... ________
i. The owner's drawing account is increased with a .... ________

Exercise 3-3A

1. and 2.

Cash

Richard Gibbs, Capital

Supplies

Utilities Expense

Exercise 3-4A

Account	Debit or Credit
1. Cash	______________
2. Wages Expense	______________
3. Accounts Payable	______________
4. Owner's Drawing	______________
5. Supplies	______________
6. Owner's Capital	______________
7. Equipment	______________

Exercises 3-5A and 3-6A: See page WP-21

Name ______________________________

Exercises 3-5A and 3-6A

Assets		=	Liabilities		+	Owner's Equity	
Dr. +	Cr. −		Dr. −	Cr. +		Dr. −	Cr. +

Drawing		Expenses		Revenues	
Dr. +	Cr. −	Dr. +	Cr. −	Dr. −	Cr. +

Exercise 3-7A

Assets		=	Liabilities		+	Owner's Equity	
Dr. +	Cr. −		Dr. −	Cr. +		Dr. −	Cr. +

Drawing		Expenses		Revenues	
Dr. +	Cr. −	Dr. +	Cr. −	Dr. −	Cr. +

Name ______________________________

Exercise 3-8A

ACCOUNT	DEBIT BALANCE	CREDIT BALANCE

Exercise 3-9A

ACCOUNT	DEBIT BALANCE	CREDIT BALANCE

Exercise 3-10A

Name ______________________________

Exercise 3-11A

Exercise 3-12A

Problem 3-13A
1. and 2.

Assets		=	Liabilities		+	Owner's Equity	
Dr. +	Cr. −		Dr. −	Cr. +		Dr. −	Cr. +

Drawing		Expenses		Revenues	
Dr. +	Cr. −	Dr. +	Cr. −	Dr. −	Cr. +

Name ______________________________

Problem 3-13A (Concluded)

3.

ACCOUNT	DEBIT BALANCE	CREDIT BALANCE

Problem 3-14A

1.

a. Total revenue for the month .... ______________

b. Total expenses for the month .... ______________

c. Net income for the month .... ______________

2.

a. Wilhelm Kohl's original investment in the business .... ______________

+ Net income for the month .... ______________

– Owner's drawing .... ______________

Increase in capital .... ______________

= Ending owner's equity .... ______________

b. End-of-month accounting equation:

Assets	=	Liabilities	+	Owner's Equity
______________		______________		______________

Problem 3-15A

1.

Name ______________________________

Problem 3-15A (Concluded)

2.

3.

Exercise 3-1B

Accounts Payable	
300	450
250	350
	150

Exercise 3-2B

a. The asset account Prepaid Insurance is increased with a .... ____________

b. The owner's drawing account is increased with a .... ____________

c. The asset account Accounts Receivable is decreased with a .... ____________

d. The liability account Accounts Payable is decreased with a .... ____________

e. The owner's capital account is increased with a .... ____________

f. The revenue account Professional Fees is increased with a .... ____________

g. The expense account Repair Expense is increased with a .... ____________

h. The asset account Cash is decreased with a .... ____________

i. The asset account Delivery Equipment is decreased with a .... ____________

Exercise 3-3B

1. and 2.

Cash	

Roberto Alvarez, Capital	

Supplies	

Utilities Expense	

Name ______________________________

Exercise 3-4B

Account	Debit or Credit
1. Cash	____________
2. Rent Expense	____________
3. Notes Payable	____________
4. Owner's Drawing	____________
5. Accounts Receivable	____________
6. Owner's Capital	____________
7. Tools	____________

Exercises 3-5B and 3-6B: See page WP-32

Exercises 3-5B and 3-6B

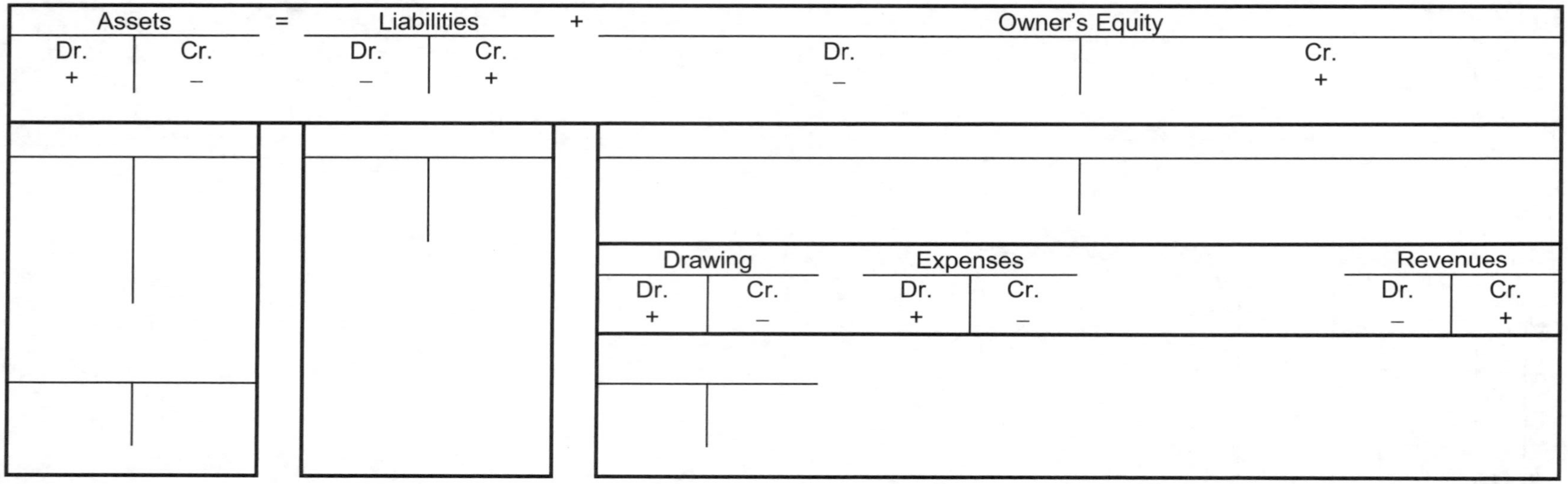

Name ______________________________

Exercise 3-7B

Assets		=	Liabilities		+	Owner's Equity	
Dr. +	Cr. −		Dr. −	Cr. +		Dr. −	Cr. +

Drawing		Expenses		Revenues	
Dr. +	Cr. −	Dr. +	Cr. −	Dr. −	Cr. +

Exercise 3-8B

ACCOUNT	DEBIT BALANCE	CREDIT BALANCE

Name ______________________________

Exercise 3-9B

ACCOUNT	DEBIT BALANCE	CREDIT BALANCE

Exercise 3-10B

Exercise 3-11B

Exercise 3-12B

Problem 3-13B
1. and 2.

Assets		=	Liabilities		+	Owner's Equity	
Dr. +	Cr. –		Dr. –	Cr. +		Dr. –	Cr. +

Drawing		Expenses		Revenues	
Dr. +	Cr. –	Dr. +	Cr. –	Dr. –	Cr. +

Problem 3-13B (Concluded)

3.

ACCOUNT	DEBIT BALANCE	CREDIT BALANCE

Problem 3-14B

1.

a. Total revenue for the month.. ______________

b. Total expenses for the month .... ______________

c. Net income for the month .... ______________

2.

a. Sue Jantz's original investment in the business .... ______________

+ Net income for the month .... ______________

– Owner's drawing .... ______________

Increase in capital .... ______________

= Ending owner's equity .... ______________

b. End-of-month accounting equation:

Assets	=	Liabilities	+	Owner's Equity
______________		______________		______________

Problem 3-15B

1.

Problem 3-15B (Concluded)

2.

3.

Mastery Problem

1. and 2.

Assets		=	Liabilities		+	Owner's Equity	
Dr. +	Cr. −		Dr. −	Cr. +		Dr. −	Cr. +

Drawing		Expenses		Revenues	
Dr. +	Cr. −	Dr. +	Cr. −	Dr. −	Cr. +

Mastery Problem (Continued)

3.

ACCOUNT	DEBIT BALANCE	CREDIT BALANCE

4.

Mastery Problem (Concluded)

5.

6.

Challenge Problem

1.

2.

Name ______________________________

Exercise 4-1A

1.	________	Check stubs or check register	a. A good or service has been sold.
2.	________	Purchase invoice from suppliers (vendors)	b. Cash has been received by the business.
3.	________	Sales tickets or invoices to customers	c. Cash has been paid by the business.
4.	________	Receipts or cash register tapes	d. Goods or services have been purchased by the business.

Exercise 4-2A

Transaction	Debit	Credit
1. Invested cash in the business, $5,000.		
2. Paid office rent, $500.		
3. Purchased office supplies on account, $300.		
4. Received cash for services rendered (fees), $400.		
5. Paid cash on account, $50.		
6. Rendered services on account, $300.		
7. Received cash for an amount owed by a customer, $100.		

Exercise 4-3A

Exercise 4-3A (Concluded)

Total Debits:	Total Credits:

Exercise 4-4A

GENERAL JOURNAL

PAGE 1

	DATE		DESCRIPTION	POST. REF.	DEBIT	CREDIT	
1							1
2							2
3							3
4							4
5							5
6							6
7							7
8							8
9							9
10							10
11							11
12							12
13							13
14							14
15							15
16							16
17							17
18							18
19							19
20							20
21							21
22							22
23							23
24							24

Exercise 4-4A (Concluded)

GENERAL JOURNAL

PAGE 2

	DATE		DESCRIPTION	POST. REF.	DEBIT	CREDIT	
1							1
2							2
3							3
4							4
5							5
6							6
7							7
8							8
9							9
10							10
11							11
12							12
13							13
14							14
15							15
16							16
17							17
18							18
19							19
20							20
21							21
22							22
23							23
24							24
25							25
26							26
27							27
28							28
29							29
30							30
31							31
32							32
33							33
34							34
35							35
36							36

Exercise 4-5A

GENERAL LEDGER

ACCOUNT ACCOUNT NO.

DATE		ITEM	POST. REF.	DEBIT	CREDIT	BALANCE DEBIT	BALANCE CREDIT

ACCOUNT ACCOUNT NO.

DATE		ITEM	POST. REF.	DEBIT	CREDIT	BALANCE DEBIT	BALANCE CREDIT

ACCOUNT ACCOUNT NO.

DATE		ITEM	POST. REF.	DEBIT	CREDIT	BALANCE DEBIT	BALANCE CREDIT

Exercise 4-5A (Continued)

ACCOUNT ACCOUNT NO.

DATE		ITEM	POST. REF.	DEBIT	CREDIT	BALANCE DEBIT	BALANCE CREDIT

ACCOUNT ACCOUNT NO.

DATE		ITEM	POST. REF.	DEBIT	CREDIT	BALANCE DEBIT	BALANCE CREDIT

ACCOUNT ACCOUNT NO.

DATE		ITEM	POST. REF.	DEBIT	CREDIT	BALANCE DEBIT	BALANCE CREDIT

ACCOUNT ACCOUNT NO.

DATE		ITEM	POST. REF.	DEBIT	CREDIT	BALANCE DEBIT	BALANCE CREDIT

Exercise 4-5A (Continued)

ACCOUNT ACCOUNT NO.

DATE	ITEM	POST. REF.	DEBIT	CREDIT	BALANCE DEBIT	BALANCE CREDIT

ACCOUNT ACCOUNT NO.

DATE	ITEM	POST. REF.	DEBIT	CREDIT	BALANCE DEBIT	BALANCE CREDIT

ACCOUNT ACCOUNT NO.

DATE	ITEM	POST. REF.	DEBIT	CREDIT	BALANCE DEBIT	BALANCE CREDIT

ACCOUNT ACCOUNT NO.

DATE	ITEM	POST. REF.	DEBIT	CREDIT	BALANCE DEBIT	BALANCE CREDIT

ACCOUNT ACCOUNT NO.

DATE	ITEM	POST. REF.	DEBIT	CREDIT	BALANCE DEBIT	BALANCE CREDIT

Exercise 4-5A (Concluded)

ACCOUNT TITLE	ACCT. NO.	DEBIT BALANCE	CREDIT BALANCE

Exercise 4-6A

Exercise 4-6A (Concluded)

Name ______________________________

Exercise 4-7A

Exercise 4-7A (Concluded)

Exercise 4-8A

GENERAL JOURNAL PAGE

	DATE		DESCRIPTION	POST. REF.	DEBIT	CREDIT	
15	May	17	Office Equipment		400 00		15
16			Cash			400 00	16
17			Purchased copy paper				17
18							18
23		23	Cash	101	1000 00		23
24			Service Fees	401		1000 00	24
25			Received cash for services previously earned				25
26							26
27							27
28							28
29							29
30							30
31							31
32							32
33							33

Name ____________________

Problem 4-9A

2. **(For 1. and 3., see page WP-58.)**

GENERAL JOURNAL

PAGE 1

DATE		DESCRIPTION	POST. REF.	DEBIT	CREDIT

Problem 4-9A (Continued)

GENERAL JOURNAL

PAGE 2

	DATE		DESCRIPTION	POST. REF.	DEBIT	CREDIT	
1							1
2							2
3							3
4							4
5							5
6							6
7							7
8							8
9							9
10							10
11							11
12							12
13							13
14							14
15							15
16							16
17							17
18							18
19							19
20							20
21							21
22							22
23							23
24							24
25							25
26							26
27							27
28							28
29							29
30							30
31							31
32							32
33							33
34							34
35							35
36							36

Problem 4-9A (Continued)

GENERAL JOURNAL

PAGE 3

DATE	DESCRIPTION	POST. REF.	DEBIT	CREDIT

Problm 4-9A (Continued)

1. and 3.

GENERAL LEDGER

ACCOUNT Cash ACCOUNT NO. 101

DATE		ITEM	POST. REF.	DEBIT	CREDIT	BALANCE	
						DEBIT	CREDIT

ACCOUNT Office Supplies ACCOUNT NO. 142

DATE		ITEM	POST. REF.	DEBIT	CREDIT	BALANCE	
						DEBIT	CREDIT

Name ______________________________

Problem 4-9A (Continued)

ACCOUNT Office Equipment ACCOUNT NO. 181

DATE		ITEM	POST. REF.	DEBIT	CREDIT	BALANCE DEBIT	BALANCE CREDIT

ACCOUNT Accounts Payable ACCOUNT NO. 202

DATE		ITEM	POST. REF.	DEBIT	CREDIT	BALANCE DEBIT	BALANCE CREDIT

ACCOUNT Annette Creighton, Capital ACCOUNT NO. 311

DATE		ITEM	POST. REF.	DEBIT	CREDIT	BALANCE DEBIT	BALANCE CREDIT

ACCOUNT Annette Creighton, Drawing ACCOUNT NO. 312

DATE		ITEM	POST. REF.	DEBIT	CREDIT	BALANCE DEBIT	BALANCE CREDIT

Problem 4-9A (Continued)

ACCOUNT Consulting Fees ACCOUNT NO. 401

DATE		ITEM	POST. REF.	DEBIT	CREDIT	BALANCE DEBIT	BALANCE CREDIT

ACCOUNT Wages Expense ACCOUNT NO. 511

DATE		ITEM	POST. REF.	DEBIT	CREDIT	BALANCE DEBIT	BALANCE CREDIT

ACCOUNT Advertising Expense ACCOUNT NO. 512

DATE		ITEM	POST. REF.	DEBIT	CREDIT	BALANCE DEBIT	BALANCE CREDIT

ACCOUNT Rent Expense ACCOUNT NO. 521

DATE		ITEM	POST. REF.	DEBIT	CREDIT	BALANCE DEBIT	BALANCE CREDIT

Name ______________________________

Problem 4-9A (Continued)

ACCOUNT Telephone Expense ACCOUNT NO. 525

DATE		ITEM	POST. REF.	DEBIT	CREDIT	BALANCE DEBIT	BALANCE CREDIT

ACCOUNT Transportation Expense ACCOUNT NO 526

DATE		ITEM	POST. REF.	DEBIT	CREDIT	BALANCE DEBIT	BALANCE CREDIT

ACCOUNT Utilities Expense ACCOUNT NO. 533

DATE		ITEM	POST. REF.	DEBIT	CREDIT	BALANCE DEBIT	BALANCE CREDIT

ACCOUNT Miscellaneous Expense ACCOUNT NO. 549

DATE		ITEM	POST. REF.	DEBIT	CREDIT	BALANCE DEBIT	BALANCE CREDIT

Problem 4-9A (Continued)

4.

ACCOUNT TITLE	ACCT. NO.	DEBIT BALANCE	CREDIT BALANCE

Problem 4-9A (Continued)

5.

Problem 4-9A (Concluded)

Name ______________________________

Problem 4-10A

2. (For 1. and 3., see page WP-68.)

GENERAL JOURNAL

PAGE 7

	DATE		DESCRIPTION	POST. REF.	DEBIT	CREDIT	
1							1
2							2
3							3
4							4
5							5
6							6
7							7
8							8
9							9
10							10
11							11
12							12
13							13
14							14
15							15
16							16
17							17
18							18
19							19
20							20
21							21
22							22
23							23
24							24
25							25
26							26
27							27
28							28
29							29
30							30
31							31
32							32
33							33
34							34

Problem 4-10A (Continued)

GENERAL JOURNAL

PAGE 8

	DATE		DESCRIPTION	POST. REF.	DEBIT	CREDIT	
1							1
2							2
3							3
4							4
5							5
6							6
7							7
8							8
9							9
10							10
11							11
12							12
13							13
14							14
15							15
16							16
17							17
18							18
19							19
20							20
21							21
22							22
23							23
24							24
25							25
26							26
27							27
28							28
29							29
30							30
31							31
32							32
33							33
34							34
35							35
36							36

Problem 4-10A (Continued)

GENERAL JOURNAL

PAGE 9

DATE		DESCRIPTION	POST. REF.	DEBIT	CREDIT

Problem 4-10A (Continued)

1. and 3.

ACCOUNT Cash **GENERAL LEDGER** ACCOUNT NO. 101

DATE		ITEM	POST. REF.	DEBIT	CREDIT	BALANCE	
						DEBIT	CREDIT

Problem 4-10A (Continued)

ACCOUNT Accounts Receivable ACCOUNT NO. 122

DATE		ITEM	POST. REF.	DEBIT	CREDIT	BALANCE DEBIT	BALANCE CREDIT

ACCOUNT Office Supplies ACCOUNT NO. 142

DATE		ITEM	POST. REF.	DEBIT	CREDIT	BALANCE DEBIT	BALANCE CREDIT

ACCOUNT Office Equipment ACCOUNT NO. 181

DATE		ITEM	POST. REF.	DEBIT	CREDIT	BALANCE DEBIT	BALANCE CREDIT

ACCOUNT Delivery Truck ACCOUNT NO. 185

DATE		ITEM	POST. REF.	DEBIT	CREDIT	BALANCE DEBIT	BALANCE CREDIT

Problem 4-10A (Continued)

ACCOUNT Accounts Payable ACCOUNT NO. 202

DATE	ITEM	POST. REF.	DEBIT	CREDIT	BALANCE DEBIT	BALANCE CREDIT

ACCOUNT Jim Andrews, Capital ACCOUNT NO. 311

DATE	ITEM	POST. REF.	DEBIT	CREDIT	BALANCE DEBIT	BALANCE CREDIT

ACCOUNT Jim Andrews, Drawing ACCOUNT NO. 312

DATE	ITEM	POST. REF.	DEBIT	CREDIT	BALANCE DEBIT	BALANCE CREDIT

ACCOUNT Delivery Fees ACCOUNT NO. 401

DATE	ITEM	POST. REF.	DEBIT	CREDIT	BALANCE DEBIT	BALANCE CREDIT

Problem 4-10A (Continued)

ACCOUNT Wages Expense ACCOUNT NO. 511

DATE		ITEM	POST. REF.	DEBIT	CREDIT	BALANCE DEBIT	BALANCE CREDIT

ACCOUNT Advertising Expense ACCOUNT NO. 512

DATE		ITEM	POST. REF.	DEBIT	CREDIT	BALANCE DEBIT	BALANCE CREDIT

ACCOUNT Rent Expense ACCOUNT NO. 521

DATE		ITEM	POST. REF.	DEBIT	CREDIT	BALANCE DEBIT	BALANCE CREDIT

ACCOUNT Telephone Expense ACCOUNT NO. 525

DATE		ITEM	POST. REF.	DEBIT	CREDIT	BALANCE DEBIT	BALANCE CREDIT

Problem 4-10A (Continued)

ACCOUNT Electricity Expense ACCOUNT NO. 533

DATE	ITEM	POST. REF.	DEBIT	CREDIT	BALANCE	
					DEBIT	CREDIT

ACCOUNT Charitable Contributions Expense ACCOUNT NO. 534

DATE	ITEM	POST. REF.	DEBIT	CREDIT	BALANCE	
					DEBIT	CREDIT

ACCOUNT Gas and Oil Expense ACCOUNT NO. 538

DATE	ITEM	POST. REF.	DEBIT	CREDIT	BALANCE	
					DEBIT	CREDIT

ACCOUNT Miscellaneous Expense ACCOUNT NO. 549

DATE	ITEM	POST. REF.	DEBIT	CREDIT	BALANCE	
					DEBIT	CREDIT

Problem 4-10A (Concluded)

4.

ACCOUNT TITLE	ACCT. NO.	DEBIT BALANCE	CREDIT BALANCE

Problem 4-11A

GENERAL JOURNAL

PAGE

	DATE		DESCRIPTION	POST. REF.	DEBIT	CREDIT	
1							1
2							2
3							3
4							4
5							5
6							6
7							7
8							8
9							9
10							10
11							11
12							12
13							13
14							14
15							15
16							16
17							17
18							18
19							19
20							20

Exercise 4-1B

1. Cash register tape
2. Sales ticket (issued to customer)
3. Purchase invoice (received from supplier or vendor)
4. Check stub

Exercise 4-2B

Transaction	Debit	Credit
1. Invested cash in the business, $1,000.		
2. Performed services on account, $200.		
3. Purchased office equipment on account, $500.		
4. Received cash on account for services previously rendered, $200.		
5. Made a payment on account, $100.		

Exercise 4-3B

Total Debits:	Total Credits:

Exercise 4-4B

GENERAL JOURNAL

PAGE 1

DATE		DESCRIPTION	POST. REF.	DEBIT	CREDIT

Exercise 4-4B (Concluded)

GENERAL JOURNAL

PAGE 2

DATE	DESCRIPTION	POST. REF.	DEBIT	CREDIT

Exercise 4-5B

GENERAL LEDGER

ACCOUNT ACCOUNT NO.

DATE		ITEM	POST. REF.	DEBIT	CREDIT	BALANCE	
						DEBIT	CREDIT

ACCOUNT ACCOUNT NO.

DATE		ITEM	POST. REF.	DEBIT	CREDIT	BALANCE	
						DEBIT	CREDIT

ACCOUNT ACCOUNT NO.

DATE		ITEM	POST. REF.	DEBIT	CREDIT	BALANCE	
						DEBIT	CREDIT

Exercise 4-5B (Continued)

ACCOUNT ACCOUNT NO.

DATE	ITEM	POST. REF.	DEBIT	CREDIT	BALANCE DEBIT	BALANCE CREDIT

ACCOUNT ACCOUNT NO.

DATE	ITEM	POST. REF.	DEBIT	CREDIT	BALANCE DEBIT	BALANCE CREDIT

ACCOUNT ACCOUNT NO.

DATE	ITEM	POST. REF.	DEBIT	CREDIT	BALANCE DEBIT	BALANCE CREDIT

ACCOUNT ACCOUNT NO.

DATE	ITEM	POST. REF.	DEBIT	CREDIT	BALANCE DEBIT	BALANCE CREDIT

Exercise 4-5B (Continued)

ACCOUNT ACCOUNT NO.

DATE	ITEM	POST. REF.	DEBIT	CREDIT	BALANCE DEBIT	BALANCE CREDIT

ACCOUNT ACCOUNT NO.

DATE	ITEM	POST. REF.	DEBIT	CREDIT	BALANCE DEBIT	BALANCE CREDIT

ACCOUNT ACCOUNT NO.

DATE	ITEM	POST. REF.	DEBIT	CREDIT	BALANCE DEBIT	BALANCE CREDIT

ACCOUNT ACCOUNT NO.

DATE	ITEM	POST. REF.	DEBIT	CREDIT	BALANCE DEBIT	BALANCE CREDIT

ACCOUNT ACCOUNT NO.

DATE	ITEM	POST. REF.	DEBIT	CREDIT	BALANCE DEBIT	BALANCE CREDIT

Exercise 4-5B (Concluded)

ACCOUNT TITLE	ACCT. NO.	DEBIT BALANCE	CREDIT BALANCE

Exercise 4-6B

Exercise 4-6B (Concluded)

Name ________________________________

Exercise 4-7B

Exercise 4-7B (Concluded)

Exercise 4-8B

GENERAL JOURNAL PAGE

DATE		DESCRIPTION	POST. REF.	DEBIT	CREDIT
Apr.	6	Office Supplies		530.00	
		Cash			530.00
		Purchased office equipment			
	21	Cash	101	300.00	
		Service Fees	401		300.00
		Revenue earned from services			
		previously rendered			

Problem 4-9B

2. **(For 1. and 3., see page WP-88.)**

GENERAL JOURNAL

PAGE 1

DATE		DESCRIPTION	POST. REF.	DEBIT	CREDIT

Problem 4-9B (Continued)

GENERAL JOURNAL

PAGE 2

DATE		DESCRIPTION	POST. REF.	DEBIT	CREDIT

Problem 4-9B (Continued)

GENERAL JOURNAL

PAGE 3

	DATE		DESCRIPTION	POST. REF.	DEBIT	CREDIT	
1							1
2							2
3							3
4							4
5							5
6							6
7							7
8							8
9							9
10							10
11							11
12							12
13							13
14							14
15							15
16							16
17							17
18							18
19							19
20							20
21							21
22							22
23							23
24							24
25							25
26							26
27							27
28							28
29							29
30							30
31							31
32							32
33							33
34							34
35							35
36							36

Problem 4-9B (Continued)

1. and 3.

GENERAL LEDGER

ACCOUNT Cash ACCOUNT NO. 101

DATE	ITEM	POST. REF.	DEBIT	CREDIT	BALANCE	
					DEBIT	CREDIT

ACCOUNT Accounts Receivable ACCOUNT NO. 122

DATE	ITEM	POST. REF.	DEBIT	CREDIT	BALANCE	
					DEBIT	CREDIT

Problem 4-9B (Continued)

ACCOUNT Office Supplies ACCOUNT NO. 142

DATE	ITEM	POST. REF.	DEBIT	CREDIT	BALANCE DEBIT	BALANCE CREDIT

ACCOUNT Office Equipment ACCOUNT NO. 181

DATE	ITEM	POST. REF.	DEBIT	CREDIT	BALANCE DEBIT	BALANCE CREDIT

ACCOUNT Accounts Payable ACCOUNT NO. 202

DATE	ITEM	POST. REF.	DEBIT	CREDIT	BALANCE DEBIT	BALANCE CREDIT

ACCOUNT Benito Mendez, Capital ACCOUNT NO. 311

DATE	ITEM	POST. REF.	DEBIT	CREDIT	BALANCE DEBIT	BALANCE CREDIT

Problem 4-9B (Continued)

ACCOUNT Benito Mendez, Drawing ACCOUNT NO. 312

DATE	ITEM	POST. REF.	DEBIT	CREDIT	BALANCE DEBIT	BALANCE CREDIT

ACCOUNT Appraisal Fees ACCOUNT NO. 401

DATE	ITEM	POST. REF.	DEBIT	CREDIT	BALANCE DEBIT	BALANCE CREDIT

ACCOUNT Wages Expense ACCOUNT NO. 511

DATE	ITEM	POST. REF.	DEBIT	CREDIT	BALANCE DEBIT	BALANCE CREDIT

ACCOUNT Advertising Expense ACCOUNT NO. 512

DATE	ITEM	POST. REF.	DEBIT	CREDIT	BALANCE DEBIT	BALANCE CREDIT

Problem 4-9B (Continued)

ACCOUNT Rent Expense ACCOUNT NO. 521

DATE	ITEM	POST. REF.	DEBIT	CREDIT	BALANCE DEBIT	BALANCE CREDIT

ACCOUNT Telephone Expense ACCOUNT NO. 525

DATE	ITEM	POST. REF.	DEBIT	CREDIT	BALANCE DEBIT	BALANCE CREDIT

ACCOUNT Transportation Expense ACCOUNT NO 526

DATE	ITEM	POST. REF.	DEBIT	CREDIT	BALANCE DEBIT	BALANCE CREDIT

ACCOUNT Electricity Expense ACCOUNT NO. 533

DATE	ITEM	POST. REF.	DEBIT	CREDIT	BALANCE DEBIT	BALANCE CREDIT

ACCOUNT Miscellaneous Expense ACCOUNT NO. 549

DATE	ITEM	POST. REF.	DEBIT	CREDIT	BALANCE DEBIT	BALANCE CREDIT

Problem 4-9B (Continued)

4.

ACCOUNT TITLE	ACCT. NO.	DEBIT BALANCE	CREDIT BALANCE

Name ______________________________

Problem 4-9B (Continued)

5.

Problem 4-9B (Concluded)

Name ______________________________

Problem 4-10B

2. **(For 1. and 3., see page WP-98.)**

GENERAL JOURNAL

PAGE 7

DATE		DESCRIPTION	POST. REF.	DEBIT	CREDIT

Problem 4-10B (Continued)

GENERAL JOURNAL

PAGE 8

	DATE		DESCRIPTION	POST. REF.	DEBIT	CREDIT	
1							1
2							2
3							3
4							4
5							5
6							6
7							7
8							8
9							9
10							10
11							11
12							12
13							13
14							14
15							15
16							16
17							17
18							18
19							19
20							20
21							21
22							22
23							23
24							24
25							25
26							26
27							27
28							28
29							29
30							30
31							31
32							32
33							33
34							34
35							35
36							36

Problem 4-10B (Continued)

GENERAL JOURNAL

PAGE 9

	DATE		DESCRIPTION	POST. REF.	DEBIT	CREDIT	
1							1
2							2
3							3
4							4
5							5
6							6
7							7
8							8
9							9
10							10
11							11
12							12
13							13
14							14
15							15
16							16
17							17
18							18
19							19
20							20
21							21
22							22
23							23
24							24
25							25
26							26
27							27
28							28
29							29
30							30
31							31
32							32
33							33
34							34
35							35
36							36

Problem 4-10B (Continued)

1. and 3.

GENERAL LEDGER

ACCOUNT Cash ACCOUNT NO. 101

DATE		ITEM	POST. REF.	DEBIT	CREDIT	BALANCE	
						DEBIT	CREDIT

ACCOUNT Accounts Receivable ACCOUNT NO. 122

DATE		ITEM	POST. REF.	DEBIT	CREDIT	BALANCE	
						DEBIT	CREDIT

Problem 4-10B (Continued)

ACCOUNT Tailoring Supplies ACCOUNT NO. 141

DATE		ITEM	POST. REF.	DEBIT	CREDIT	BALANCE DEBIT	BALANCE CREDIT

ACCOUNT Tailoring Equipment ACCOUNT NO. 183

DATE		ITEM	POST. REF.	DEBIT	CREDIT	BALANCE DEBIT	BALANCE CREDIT

ACCOUNT Accounts Payable ACCOUNT NO. 202

DATE		ITEM	POST. REF.	DEBIT	CREDIT	BALANCE DEBIT	BALANCE CREDIT

ACCOUNT Ann Taylor, Capital ACCOUNT NO. 311

DATE		ITEM	POST. REF.	DEBIT	CREDIT	BALANCE DEBIT	BALANCE CREDIT

Problem 4-10B (Continued)

ACCOUNT Ann Taylor, Drawing ACCOUNT NO. 312

DATE	ITEM	POST. REF.	DEBIT	CREDIT	BALANCE DEBIT	BALANCE CREDIT

ACCOUNT Tailoring Fees ACCOUNT NO. 401

DATE	ITEM	POST. REF.	DEBIT	CREDIT	BALANCE DEBIT	BALANCE CREDIT

ACCOUNT Wages Expense ACCOUNT NO. 511

DATE	ITEM	POST. REF.	DEBIT	CREDIT	BALANCE DEBIT	BALANCE CREDIT

ACCOUNT Advertising Expense ACCOUNT NO. 512

DATE	ITEM	POST. REF.	DEBIT	CREDIT	BALANCE DEBIT	BALANCE CREDIT

Problem 4-10B (Continued)

ACCOUNT Rent Expense ACCOUNT NO. 521

DATE		ITEM	POST. REF.	DEBIT	CREDIT	BALANCE DEBIT	BALANCE CREDIT

ACCOUNT Telephone Expense ACCOUNT NO. 525

DATE		ITEM	POST. REF.	DEBIT	CREDIT	BALANCE DEBIT	BALANCE CREDIT

ACCOUNT Electricity Expense ACCOUNT NO. 533

DATE		ITEM	POST. REF.	DEBIT	CREDIT	BALANCE DEBIT	BALANCE CREDIT

ACCOUNT Miscellaneous Expense ACCOUNT NO. 549

DATE		ITEM	POST. REF.	DEBIT	CREDIT	BALANCE DEBIT	BALANCE CREDIT

Problem 4-10B (Concluded)

4.

ACCOUNT TITLE	ACCT. NO.	DEBIT BALANCE	CREDIT BALANCE

Problem 4-11B

GENERAL JOURNAL

PAGE

DATE		DESCRIPTION	POST. REF.	DEBIT	CREDIT

Mastery Problem

1.

GENERAL JOURNAL

PAGE 1

	DATE		DESCRIPTION	POST. REF.	DEBIT	CREDIT	
1							1
2							2
3							3
4							4
5							5
6							6
7							7
8							8
9							9
10							10
11							11
12							12
13							13
14							14
15							15
16							16
17							17
18							18
19							19
20							20
21							21
22							22
23							23
24							24
25							25
26							26
27							27
28							28
29							29
30							30
31							31
32							32
33							33
34							34
35							35

Mastery Problem (Continued)

GENERAL JOURNAL

PAGE 2

	DATE		DESCRIPTION	POST. REF.	DEBIT	CREDIT	
1							1
2							2
3							3
4							4
5							5
6							6
7							7
8							8
9							9
10							10
11							11
12							12
13							13
14							14
15							15
16							16
17							17
18							18
19							19
20							20
21							21
22							22
23							23
24							24
25							25
26							26
27							27
28							28
29							29
30							30
31							31
32							32
33							33
34							34
35							35

Mastery Problem (Continued)

GENERAL JOURNAL

PAGE 3

	DATE	DESCRIPTION	POST. REF.	DEBIT	CREDIT	
1						1
2						2
3						3
4						4
5						5
6						6
7						7
8						8
9						9
10						10
11						11
12						12
13						13
14						14
15						15
16						16
17						17
18						18
19						19
20						20
21						21
22						22
23						23
24						24
25						25
26						26
27						27
28						28
29						29
30						30
31						31
32						32
33						33
34						34
35						35

Name ____________________________

Mastery Problem (Continued)

2.

GENERAL LEDGER

ACCOUNT Cash ACCOUNT NO. 101

DATE		ITEM	POST. REF.	DEBIT	CREDIT	BALANCE	
						DEBIT	CREDIT

ACCOUNT Office Supplies ACCOUNT NO. 142

DATE		ITEM	POST. REF.	DEBIT	CREDIT	BALANCE	
						DEBIT	CREDIT

ACCOUNT Athletic Equipment ACCOUNT NO. 183

DATE		ITEM	POST. REF.	DEBIT	CREDIT	BALANCE	
						DEBIT	CREDIT

Mastery Problem (Continued)

ACCOUNT Basketball Facilities ACCOUNT NO. 184

DATE		ITEM	POST. REF.	DEBIT	CREDIT	BALANCE DEBIT	BALANCE CREDIT

ACCOUNT Accounts Payable ACCOUNT NO. 202

DATE		ITEM	POST. REF.	DEBIT	CREDIT	BALANCE DEBIT	BALANCE CREDIT

ACCOUNT Barry Bird, Capital ACCOUNT NO. 311

DATE		ITEM	POST. REF.	DEBIT	CREDIT	BALANCE DEBIT	BALANCE CREDIT

ACCOUNT Barry Bird, Drawing ACCOUNT NO. 312

DATE		ITEM	POST. REF.	DEBIT	CREDIT	BALANCE DEBIT	BALANCE CREDIT

Name ______________________________

Mastery Problem (Continued)

ACCOUNT Registration Fees ACCOUNT NO. 401

DATE		ITEM	POST. REF.	DEBIT	CREDIT	BALANCE DEBIT	BALANCE CREDIT

ACCOUNT Wages Expense ACCOUNT NO. 511

DATE		ITEM	POST. REF.	DEBIT	CREDIT	BALANCE DEBIT	BALANCE CREDIT

ACCOUNT Advertising Expense ACCOUNT NO. 512

DATE		ITEM	POST. REF.	DEBIT	CREDIT	BALANCE DEBIT	BALANCE CREDIT

Mastery Problem (Continued)

ACCOUNT Food Expense ACCOUNT NO. 524

DATE	ITEM	POST. REF.	DEBIT	CREDIT	BALANCE DEBIT	BALANCE CREDIT

ACCOUNT Telephone Expense ACCOUNT NO. 525

DATE	ITEM	POST. REF.	DEBIT	CREDIT	BALANCE DEBIT	BALANCE CREDIT

ACCOUNT Utilities Expense ACCOUNT NO. 533

DATE	ITEM	POST. REF.	DEBIT	CREDIT	BALANCE DEBIT	BALANCE CREDIT

ACCOUNT Postage Expense ACCOUNT NO. 536

DATE	ITEM	POST. REF.	DEBIT	CREDIT	BALANCE DEBIT	BALANCE CREDIT

Mastery Problem (Concluded)

3.

ACCOUNT TITLE	ACCT. NO.	DEBIT BALANCE	CREDIT BALANCE

Challenge Problem

1. and 2.

3.

Fred Phaler Consulting
Trial Balance
June 30, 20--

ACCOUNT TITLE	ACCT. NO.	DEBIT BALANCE	CREDIT BALANCE
Cash	101		
Accounts Receivable	122		
Office Supplies	142		
Accounts Payable	202		
Fred Phaler, Capital	311		
Fred Phaler, Drawing	312		
Professional Fees	401		
Wages Expense	511		
Rent Expense	521		
Telephone Expense	525		
Automobile Expense	526		
Utilities Expense	533		

Exercise 5-1A

(Balance Sheet) Supplies	

(Income Statement) Supplies Expense	

GENERAL JOURNAL

PAGE

	DATE		DESCRIPTION	POST. REF.	DEBIT	CREDIT	
1							1
2							2
3							3
4							4
5							5
6							6

Exercise 5-2A

(Balance Sheet) Prepaid Insurance	

(Income Statement) Insurance Expense	

GENERAL JOURNAL

PAGE

	DATE		DESCRIPTION	POST. REF.	DEBIT	CREDIT	
1							1
2							2
3							3
4							4
5							5
6							6

Exercise 5-3A

(Income Statement) Wages Expense	

(Balance Sheet) Wages Payable	

GENERAL JOURNAL PAGE

	DATE		DESCRIPTION	POST. REF.	DEBIT	CREDIT	
1							1
2							2
3							3
4							4

Exercise 5-4A

(Income Statement) Depr. Expense—Delivery Equipment	

(Balance Sheet) Accum. Depr.—Delivery Equipment	

GENERAL JOURNAL PAGE

	DATE		DESCRIPTION	POST. REF.	DEBIT	CREDIT	
1							1
2							2
3							3
4							4

Exercise 5-5A

Exercise 5-6A

1.

(Balance Sheet) Supplies		(Income Statement) Supplies Expense	
TB 580			
Bal. ______			

2.

(Balance Sheet) Supplies		(Income Statement) Supplies Expense	
TB 435			
Bal. ______			

Exercise 5-7A

1.

(Balance Sheet) Prepaid Insurance		(Income Statement) Insurance Expense	
TB 1,450			
Bal. ______			

2.

(Balance Sheet) Prepaid Insurance		(Income Statement) Insurance Expense	
TB 1,350			
Bal. ______			

Exercise 5-8A

GENERAL JOURNAL

PAGE 9

DATE		DESCRIPTION	POST. REF.	DEBIT	CREDIT
		Adjusting Entries			
20-- Dec.	31	Supplies Expense		85 00	
		Supplies			85 00
	31	Wages Expense		220 00	
		Wages Payable			220 00

Name ________________________________

Exercise 5-8A (Concluded)

GENERAL LEDGER

ACCOUNT Supplies ACCOUNT NO. 141

DATE		ITEM	POST. REF.	DEBIT	CREDIT	BALANCE DEBIT	BALANCE CREDIT
20-- Dec.	1	Balance	✓			150.00	
	15		J8	50.00		200.00	

ACCOUNT Wages Payable ACCOUNT NO. 219

DATE		ITEM	POST. REF.	DEBIT	CREDIT	BALANCE DEBIT	BALANCE CREDIT

ACCOUNT Wages Expense ACCOUNT NO. 511

DATE		ITEM	POST. REF.	DEBIT	CREDIT	BALANCE DEBIT	BALANCE CREDIT
20-- Dec.	1	Balance	✓			900.00	
	15		J8	300.00		1200.00	

ACCOUNT Supplies Expense ACCOUNT NO. 523

DATE		ITEM	POST. REF.	DEBIT	CREDIT	BALANCE DEBIT	BALANCE CREDIT

Exercise 5-9A

Jim Jacobs' Furniture Repair
Work Sheet (Partial)
For Year Ended December 31, 20--

	ACCOUNT TITLE	TRIAL BALANCE DEBIT	TRIAL BALANCE CREDIT	ADJUSTMENTS DEBIT	ADJUSTMENTS CREDIT	ADJUSTED TRIAL BALANCE DEBIT	ADJUSTED TRIAL BALANCE CREDIT	
1	Cash	100.00				100.00		1
2	Supplies	850.00				200.00		2
3	Prepaid Insurance	900.00				300.00		3
4	Delivery Equipment	3600.00				3600.00		4
5	Accum. Depr.—Delivery Equip.		600.00				800.00	5
6	Wages Payable						100.00	6
7	Jim Jacobs, Capital		4000.00				4000.00	7
8	Repair Fees		1650.00				1650.00	8
9	Wages Expense	600.00				700.00		9
10	Advertising Expense	200.00				200.00		10
11	Supplies Expense					650.00		11
12	Insurance Expense					600.00		12
13	Depr. Exp.—Delivery Equip.					200.00		13
14		6250.00	6250.00			6550.00	6550.00	14
15								15
16								16
17								17
18								18
19								19
20								20
21								21
22								22
23								23
24								24
25								25

Name ______________________________

Exercise 5-10A

GENERAL JOURNAL

PAGE

	DATE		DESCRIPTION	POST. REF.	DEBIT	CREDIT	
1							1
2							2
3							3
4							4
5							5
6							6
7							7
8							8
9							9
10							10
11							11
12							12
13							13
14							14
15							15

Exercise 5-11A

	Income Statement		Balance Sheet	
	Debit	**Credit**	**Debit**	**Credit**
Cash				
Accounts Receivable				
Supplies				
Prepaid Insurance				
Delivery Equipment				
Accum. Depr.—Delivery Equip.				
Accounts Payable				
Wages Payable				
Owner, Capital				
Owner, Drawing				
Delivery Fees				
Wages Expense				
Rent Expense				
Supplies Expense				
Insurance Expense				
Depr. Exp.—Delivery Equip.				

Exercise 5-12A

	Income Statement		Balance Sheet	
	Debit	**Credit**	**Debit**	**Credit**
Net Income				
Net Loss				

Exercise 5-13A

	Cash Basis	Modified Cash Basis	Accrual Basis
1. Purchase supplies on account.			
2. Make payment on asset previously purchased.			
3. Purchase supplies for cash.			
4. Purchase insurance for cash.			
5. Pay cash for wages.			
6. Pay cash for telephone expense.			
7. Pay cash for new equipment.			
8. Wages earned but not paid.			
9. Prepaid item purchased, partly used.			
10. Depreciation on long-term assets.			

Problem 5-14A

Mason's Delivery

Work

For Month Ended

	ACCOUNT TITLE	TRIAL BALANCE DEBIT	TRIAL BALANCE CREDIT	ADJUSTMENTS DEBIT	ADJUSTMENTS CREDIT
1	Cash	1 6 0 0 00			
2	Accounts Receivable	9 4 0 00			
3	Supplies	6 3 5 00			
4	Prepaid Insurance	1 2 0 0 00			
5	Delivery Equipment	6 4 0 0 00			
6	Accum. Depr.—Delivery Equip.				
7	Accounts Payable		1 2 2 0 00		
8	Wages Payable				
9	Jill Mason, Capital		8 0 0 0 00		
10	Jill Mason, Drawing	1 4 0 0 00			
11	Delivery Fees		6 2 0 0 00		
12	Wages Expense	1 5 0 0 00			
13	Advertising Expense	4 6 0 00			
14	Rent Expense	8 0 0 00			
15	Supplies Expense				
16	Telephone Expense	1 6 5 00			
17	Insurance Expense				
18	Repair Expense	2 3 0 00			
19	Oil and Gas Expense	9 0 00			
20	Depr. Exp.—Delivery Equip.				
21		15 4 2 0 00	15 4 2 0 00		
22					
23					
24					
25					
26					
27					
28					
29					
30					
31					
32					
33					

Problem 5-14A (Concluded)

Service

Sheet

September 30, 20--

ADJUSTED TRIAL BALANCE		INCOME STATEMENT		BALANCE SHEET		
DEBIT	CREDIT	DEBIT	CREDIT	DEBIT	CREDIT	
						1
						2
						3
						4
						5
						6
						7
						8
						9
						10
						11
						12
						13
						14
						15
						16
						17
						18
						19
						20
						21
						22
						23
						24
						25
						26
						27
						28
						29
						30
						31
						32
						33

Problem 5-15A

Campus Delivery

Work

For Month Ended

	ACCOUNT TITLE	TRIAL BALANCE		ADJUSTMENTS	
		DEBIT	CREDIT	DEBIT	CREDIT
1	Cash	980 00			
2	Accounts Receivable	590 00			
3	Supplies	575 00			
4	Prepaid Insurance	1300 00			
5	Van	5800 00			
6	Accumulated Depreciation—Van				
7	Accounts Payable		960 00		
8	Wages Payable				
9	Jason Armstrong, Capital		10000 00		
10	Jason Armstrong, Drawing	600 00			
11	Delivery Fees		2600 00		
12	Wages Expense	1800 00			
13	Advertising Expense	380 00			
14	Rent Expense	900 00			
15	Supplies Expense				
16	Telephone Expense	220 00			
17	Insurance Expense				
18	Repair Expense	315 00			
19	Oil and Gas Expense	100 00			
20	Depreciation Expense—Van				
21		13560 00	13560 00		
22					
23					
24					
25					
26					
27					
28					
29					
30					
31					
32					
33					

Name ______________________________

Problem 5-15A (Concluded)

Service

Sheet

November 30, 20--

ADJUSTED TRIAL BALANCE		INCOME STATEMENT		BALANCE SHEET	
DEBIT	CREDIT	DEBIT	CREDIT	DEBIT	CREDIT

Problem 5-16A

1. **GENERAL JOURNAL** PAGE 5

DATE		DESCRIPTION	POST. REF.	DEBIT	CREDIT

Name ______________________________

Problem 5-16A (Continued)

2.

GENERAL LEDGER

ACCOUNT Supplies ACCOUNT NO. 141

DATE		ITEM	POST. REF.	DEBIT	CREDIT	BALANCE DEBIT	BALANCE CREDIT
20-- Nov.	1		J1	475.00		475.00	
	15		J4	100.00		575.00	

ACCOUNT Prepaid Insurance ACCOUNT NO. 145

DATE		ITEM	POST. REF.	DEBIT	CREDIT	BALANCE DEBIT	BALANCE CREDIT
20-- Nov.	1		J1	1,300.00		1,300.00	

ACCOUNT Accumulated Depreciation—Van ACCOUNT NO. 185.1

DATE		ITEM	POST. REF.	DEBIT	CREDIT	BALANCE DEBIT	BALANCE CREDIT

ACCOUNT Wages Payable ACCOUNT NO. 219

DATE		ITEM	POST. REF.	DEBIT	CREDIT	BALANCE DEBIT	BALANCE CREDIT

Problem 5-16A (Concluded)

GENERAL LEDGER

ACCOUNT Wages Expense ACCOUNT NO. 511

DATE		ITEM	POST. REF.	DEBIT	CREDIT	BALANCE DEBIT	BALANCE CREDIT
20-- Nov.	15		J3	900 00		900 00	
	26		J4	900 00		1800 00	

ACCOUNT Supplies Expense ACCOUNT NO. 523

DATE		ITEM	POST. REF.	DEBIT	CREDIT	BALANCE DEBIT	BALANCE CREDIT

ACCOUNT Insurance Expense ACCOUNT NO. 535

DATE		ITEM	POST. REF.	DEBIT	CREDIT	BALANCE DEBIT	BALANCE CREDIT

ACCOUNT Depreciation Expense—Van ACCOUNT NO. 541

DATE		ITEM	POST. REF.	DEBIT	CREDIT	BALANCE DEBIT	BALANCE CREDIT

Name ______________________________

Problem 5-17A: See pages 130 and 131

Exercise 5-1B

(Balance Sheet)
Supplies

(Income Statement)
Supplies Expense

GENERAL JOURNAL PAGE

	DATE		DESCRIPTION	POST. REF.	DEBIT	CREDIT	
1							1
2							2
3							3
4							4
5							5
6							6

Exercise 5-2B

(Balance Sheet)
Prepaid Insurance

(Income Statement)
Insurance Expense

GENERAL JOURNAL PAGE

	DATE		DESCRIPTION	POST. REF.	DEBIT	CREDIT	
1							1
2							2
3							3
4							4
5							5
6							6

Problem 5-17A

Joyce Lee's

Work

For Month Ended

	ACCOUNT TITLE	TRIAL BALANCE DEBIT	TRIAL BALANCE CREDIT	ADJUSTMENTS DEBIT	ADJUSTMENTS CREDIT
1	Cash	1,725.00			
2	Accounts Receivable	960.00			
3	Supplies	525.00			
4	Prepaid Insurance	930.00			
5	Office Equipment	5,450.00			
6	Accum. Depr.—Office Equipment				
7	Accounts Payable		480.00		
8	Wages Payable				
9	Joyce Lee, Capital		7,500.00		
10	Joyce Lee, Drawing	1,125.00			
11	Professional Fees		5,700.00		
12	Wages Expense	1,420.00			
13	Advertising Expense	350.00			
14	Rent Expense	700.00			
15	Supplies Expense				
16	Telephone Expense	130.00			
17	Utilities Expense	190.00			
18	Insurance Expense				
19	Depr. Expense—Office Equipment				
20	Miscellaneous Expense	175.00			
21		13,680.00	13,680.00		
22					
23					
24					
25					
26					
27					
28					
29					
30					
31					

Problem 5-17A (Concluded)

Tax Service

Sheet

March 31, 20--

ADJUSTED TRIAL BALANCE		INCOME STATEMENT		BALANCE SHEET		
DEBIT	CREDIT	DEBIT	CREDIT	DEBIT	CREDIT	
						1
						2
						3
						4
						5
						6
						7
						8
						9
						10
						11
						12
						13
						14
						15
						16
						17
						18
						19
						20
						21
						22
						23
						24
						25
						26
						27
						28
						29
						30
						31

Exercise 5-3B

(Income Statement) Wages Expense	

(Balance Sheet) Wages Payable	

GENERAL JOURNAL PAGE

	DATE		DESCRIPTION	POST. REF.	DEBIT	CREDIT	
1							1
2							2
3							3
4							4

Exercise 5-4B

(Income Statement) Depr. Expense—Delivery Equipment	

(Balance Sheet) Accum. Depr.—Delivery Equipment	

GENERAL JOURNAL PAGE

	DATE		DESCRIPTION	POST. REF.	DEBIT	CREDIT	
1							1
2							2
3							3
4							4

Exercise 5-5B

Exercise 5-6B

1.

(Balance Sheet)
Supplies

TB	540	
Bal.	______	

(Income Statement)
Supplies Expense

2.

(Balance Sheet)
Supplies

TB	330	
Bal.	______	

(Income Statement)
Supplies Expense

Exercise 5-7B

1.

(Balance Sheet)
Prepaid Insurance

TB	960	
Bal.	______	

(Income Statement)
Insurance Expense

2.

(Balance Sheet)
Prepaid Insurance

TB	1,135	
Bal.	______	

(Income Statement)
Insurance Expense

Exercise 5-8B

GENERAL JOURNAL

PAGE 7

	DATE		DESCRIPTION	POST. REF.	DEBIT	CREDIT	
1			Adjusting Entries				1
2	20-- July	31	Insurance Expense		320 00		2
3			Prepaid Insurance			320 00	3
4							4
5		31	Depreciation Expense—Cleaning Equipment		145 00		5
6			Accumulated Depreciation—Cleaning Equipment			145 00	6
7							7
8							8
9							9
10							10
11							11
12							12
13							13
14							14
15							15
16							16

Name ______________________________

Exercise 5-8B (Concluded)

GENERAL LEDGER

ACCOUNT Prepaid Insurance ACCOUNT NO. 145

DATE		ITEM	POST. REF.	DEBIT	CREDIT	BALANCE DEBIT	BALANCE CREDIT
20-- July	1	Balance	✓			320 00	
	15		J6	640 00		960 00	

ACCOUNT Accumulated Depreciation—Cleaning Equipment ACCOUNT NO. 183.1

DATE		ITEM	POST. REF.	DEBIT	CREDIT	BALANCE DEBIT	BALANCE CREDIT
20-- July	1	Balance	✓				870 00

ACCOUNT Insurance Expense ACCOUNT NO. 535

DATE		ITEM	POST. REF.	DEBIT	CREDIT	BALANCE DEBIT	BALANCE CREDIT

ACCOUNT Depreciation Expense—Cleaning Equipment ACCOUNT NO. 541

DATE		ITEM	POST. REF.	DEBIT	CREDIT	BALANCE DEBIT	BALANCE CREDIT

Exercise 5-9B

Jasmine Kah's Auto Detailing
Work Sheet (Partial)
For Month Ended June 30, 20--

ACCOUNT TITLE	TRIAL BALANCE		ADJUSTMENTS		ADJUSTED TRIAL BALANCE	
	DEBIT	CREDIT	DEBIT	CREDIT	DEBIT	CREDIT
Cash	150 00				150 00	
Supplies	520 00				90 00	
Prepaid Insurance	750 00				200 00	
Cleaning Equipment	5400 00				5400 00	
Accum. Depr.—Cleaning Equip.		850 00				1150 00
Wages Payable						250 00
Jasmine Kah, Capital		4600 00				4600 00
Detailing Fees		2220 00				2220 00
Wages Expense	700 00				950 00	
Advertising Expense	150 00				150 00	
Supplies Expense					430 00	
Insurance Expense					550 00	
Depr. Exp.—Cleaning Equip.					300 00	
	7670 00	7670 00			8220 00	8220 00

Exercise 5-10B

GENERAL JOURNAL

PAGE

	DATE		DESCRIPTION	POST. REF.	DEBIT	CREDIT	
1							1
2							2
3							3
4							4
5							5
6							6
7							7
8							8
9							9
10							10
11							11
12							12
13							13
14							14
15							15

Exercise 5-11B

	Income Statement Debit	Income Statement Credit	Balance Sheet Debit	Balance Sheet Credit
Cash				
Accounts Receivable				
Supplies				
Prepaid Insurance				
Automobile				
Accum. Depr.—Automobile				
Accounts Payable				
Wages Payable				
Owner, Capital				
Owner, Drawing				
Service Fees				
Wages Expense				
Supplies Expense				
Utilities Expense				
Insurance Expense				
Depr. Exp.—Automobile				

Exercise 5-12B

	Income Statement Debit	Income Statement Credit	Balance Sheet Debit	Balance Sheet Credit
Net Income				
Net Loss				

Name ______________________________

Exercise 5-13B

	Cash Basis	Modified Cash Basis	Accrual Basis
1. Office Equipment Cash Purchased equipment for cash			
2. Office Equipment Accounts Payable Purchased equipment on account			
3. Cash Revenue Cash receipts for week			
4. Accounts Receivable Revenue Services performed on account			
5. Prepaid Insurance Cash Purchased prepaid asset			
6. Supplies Accounts Payable Purchased prepaid asset			
7. Telephone Expense Cash Paid telephone bill			
8. Wages Expense Cash Paid wages for month			
9. Accounts Payable Cash Made payment on account			
10. Supplies Expense Supplies			

Exercise 5-13B (Concluded)

	Cash Basis	Modified Cash Basis	Accrual Basis
11. Wages Expense Wages Payable			
12. Depreciation Expense—Office Equipment Accum. Depr.—Office Equipment			

This page intentionally left blank.

Problem 5-14B

Louie's Lawn

Work

For Month Ended

	ACCOUNT TITLE	TRIAL BALANCE DEBIT	TRIAL BALANCE CREDIT	ADJUSTMENTS DEBIT	ADJUSTMENTS CREDIT
1	Cash	1,375 00			
2	Accounts Receivable	880 00			
3	Supplies	490 00			
4	Prepaid Insurance	800 00			
5	Lawn Equipment	5,700 00			
6	Accum. Depr.—Lawn Equipment				
7	Accounts Payable		780 00		
8	Wages Payable				
9	Louie Long, Capital		6,500 00		
10	Louie Long, Drawing	1,250 00			
11	Lawn Service Fees		6,100 00		
12	Wages Expense	1,145 00			
13	Advertising Expense	540 00			
14	Rent Expense	725 00			
15	Supplies Expense				
16	Telephone Expense	160 00			
17	Insurance Expense				
18	Repair Expense	250 00			
19	Depr. Expense—Lawn Equipment				
20	Miscellaneous Expense	65 00			
21		13,380 00	13,380 00		
22					
23					
24					
25					
26					
27					
28					
29					
30					
31					
32					
33					

Problem 5-14B (Concluded)

Service

Sheet

March 31, 20--

ADJUSTED TRIAL BALANCE		INCOME STATEMENT		BALANCE SHEET		
DEBIT	CREDIT	DEBIT	CREDIT	DEBIT	CREDIT	
						1
						2
						3
						4
						5
						6
						7
						8
						9
						10
						11
						12
						13
						14
						15
						16
						17
						18
						19
						20
						21
						22
						23
						24
						25
						26
						27
						28
						29
						30
						31
						32
						33

Problem 5-15B

Nolan's Home

Work

For Month Ended

	ACCOUNT TITLE	TRIAL BALANCE DEBIT	TRIAL BALANCE CREDIT	ADJUSTMENTS DEBIT	ADJUSTMENTS CREDIT
1	Cash	830 00			
2	Accounts Receivable	760 00			
3	Supplies	625 00			
4	Prepaid Insurance	950 00			
5	Automobile	6500 00			
6	Accum. Depr.—Automobile				
7	Accounts Payable		1500 00		
8	Wages Payable				
9	Val Nolan, Capital		9900 00		
10	Val Nolan, Drawing	1100 00			
11	Appraisal Fees		3000 00		
12	Wages Expense	1560 00			
13	Advertising Expense	420 00			
14	Rent Expense	1050 00			
15	Supplies Expense				
16	Telephone Expense	255 00			
17	Insurance Expense				
18	Repair Expense	270 00			
19	Oil and Gas Expense	80 00			
20	Depr. Expense—Automobile				
21		14400 00	14400 00		
22					
23					
24					
25					
26					
27					
28					
29					
30					
31					
32					
33					

Problem 5-15B (Concluded)

Appraisals

Sheet

October 31, 20--

ADJUSTED TRIAL BALANCE		INCOME STATEMENT		BALANCE SHEET	
DEBIT	CREDIT	DEBIT	CREDIT	DEBIT	CREDIT

Problem 5-16B

1. **GENERAL JOURNAL** PAGE 3

DATE		DESCRIPTION	POST. REF.	DEBIT	CREDIT

Name ______________________________

Problem 5-16B (Continued)

2.

GENERAL LEDGER

ACCOUNT Supplies ACCOUNT NO. 141

DATE		ITEM	POST. REF.	DEBIT	CREDIT	BALANCE DEBIT	BALANCE CREDIT
20-- Oct.	2		J1	625 00		625 00	

ACCOUNT Prepaid Insurance ACCOUNT NO. 145

DATE		ITEM	POST. REF.	DEBIT	CREDIT	BALANCE DEBIT	BALANCE CREDIT
20-- Oct.	3		J1	950 00		950 00	

ACCOUNT Accumulated Depreciation—Automobile ACCOUNT NO. 185.1

DATE		ITEM	POST. REF.	DEBIT	CREDIT	BALANCE DEBIT	BALANCE CREDIT

Problem 5-16B (Continued)

ACCOUNT Wages Payable ACCOUNT NO. 219

DATE		ITEM	POST. REF.	DEBIT	CREDIT	BALANCE DEBIT	BALANCE CREDIT

ACCOUNT Wages Expense ACCOUNT NO. 511

DATE		ITEM	POST. REF.	DEBIT	CREDIT	BALANCE DEBIT	BALANCE CREDIT
20-- Oct.	15		J2	700 00		700 00	
	26		J2	860 00		1560 00	

ACCOUNT Supplies Expense ACCOUNT NO. 523

DATE		ITEM	POST. REF.	DEBIT	CREDIT	BALANCE DEBIT	BALANCE CREDIT

Problem 5-16B (Concluded)

ACCOUNT Insurance Expense ACCOUNT NO. 535

DATE		ITEM	POST. REF.	DEBIT	CREDIT	BALANCE	
						DEBIT	CREDIT

ACCOUNT Depreciation Expense—Automobile ACCOUNT NO. 541

DATE		ITEM	POST. REF.	DEBIT	CREDIT	BALANCE	
						DEBIT	CREDIT

Problem 5-17B

Dick Ady's

Work

For Month Ended

	ACCOUNT TITLE	TRIAL BALANCE DEBIT	TRIAL BALANCE CREDIT	ADJUSTMENTS DEBIT	ADJUSTMENTS CREDIT
1	Cash	1,365.00			
2	Accounts Receivable	845.00			
3	Supplies	620.00			
4	Prepaid Insurance	1,150.00			
5	Office Equipment	6,400.00			
6	Accum. Depr.—Office Equipment				
7	Accounts Payable		735.00		
8	Wages Payable				
9	Dick Ady, Capital		7,800.00		
10	Dick Ady, Drawing	1,200.00			
11	Professional Fees		6,350.00		
12	Wages Expense	1,495.00			
13	Advertising Expense	380.00			
14	Rent Expense	850.00			
15	Supplies Expense				
16	Telephone Expense	205.00			
17	Utilities Expense	285.00			
18	Insurance Expense				
19	Depr. Expense—Office Equipment				
20	Miscellaneous Expense	90.00			
21		14,885.00	14,885.00		
22					
23					
24					
25					
26					
27					
28					
29					
30					
31					
32					

Name ______________________________

Problem 5-17B (Concluded)

Bookkeeping Service

Sheet

July 31, 20--

ADJUSTED TRIAL BALANCE		INCOME STATEMENT		BALANCE SHEET		
DEBIT	CREDIT	DEBIT	CREDIT	DEBIT	CREDIT	
						1
						2
						3
						4
						5
						6
						7
						8
						9
						10
						11
						12
						13
						14
						15
						16
						17
						18
						19
						20
						21
						22
						23
						24
						25
						26
						27
						28
						29
						30
						31
						32

Mastery Problem

1.

Kristi Williams Family

Work

For Year Ended

	ACCOUNT TITLE	TRIAL BALANCE DEBIT	TRIAL BALANCE CREDIT	ADJUSTMENTS DEBIT	ADJUSTMENTS CREDIT
1	Cash	8,730.00			
2	Office Supplies	700.00			
3	Prepaid Insurance	600.00			
4	Office Equipment	18,000.00			
5					
6	Computer Equipment	6,000.00			
7					
8	Notes Payable		8,000.00		
9	Accounts Payable		500.00		
10	Kristi Williams, Capital		11,400.00		
11	Kristi Williams, Drawing	3,000.00			
12	Client Fees		35,800.00		
13	Wages Expense	9,500.00			
14	Rent Expense	6,000.00			
15					
16	Utilities Expense	2,170.00			
17					
18					
19					
20	Miscellaneous Expense	1,000.00			
21		55,700.00	55,700.00		
22					
23					
24					
25					
26					
27					
28					
29					
30					
31					
32					

Mastery Problem (Continued)

Counseling Services

Sheet

December 31, 20--

ADJUSTED TRIAL BALANCE		INCOME STATEMENT		BALANCE SHEET		
DEBIT	CREDIT	DEBIT	CREDIT	DEBIT	CREDIT	
						1
						2
						3
						4
						5
						6
						7
						8
						9
						10
						11
						12
						13
						14
						15
						16
						17
						18
						19
						20
						21
						22
						23
						24
						25
						26
						27
						28
						29
						30
						31
						32

Mastery Problem (Concluded)

2.

GENERAL JOURNAL

PAGE

	DATE	DESCRIPTION	POST. REF.	DEBIT	CREDIT	
1						1
2						2
3						3
4						4
5						5
6						6
7						7
8						8
9						9
10						10
11						11
12						12
13						13
14						14
15						15
16						16
17						17
18						18
19						19
20						20
21						21
22						22
23						23
24						24
25						25
26						26
27						27
28						28
29						29
30						30
31						31
32						32
33						33
34						34
35						35

Name ______________________________

Challenge Problem

See pages 156–157 for work sheet for Challenge Problem.

Challenge Problem

1.

Diane Kiefner's Wilderness

Work

For Summer

	ACCOUNT TITLE	TRIAL BALANCE DEBIT	TRIAL BALANCE CREDIT	ADJUSTMENTS DEBIT	ADJUSTMENTS CREDIT
1	Cash	11 5 0 0 00			
2					
3					
4					
5	Diane Kiefner, Capital		15 0 0 0 00		
6	Tour Revenue		10 0 0 0 00		
7	Advertising Supplies Expense	1 0 0 0 00			
8	Food Expense	2 0 0 0 00			
9	Equipment Rental Expense	3 0 0 0 00			
10	Travel Expense	4 0 0 0 00			
11	Kayak Expense	3 5 0 0 00			
12					
13		25 0 0 0 00	25 0 0 0 00		
14					
15					
16					
17					
18					
19					

Challenge Problem (Concluded)

Kayaking Tours

Sheet

Ended 20--

ADJUSTED TRIAL BALANCE		INCOME STATEMENT		BALANCE SHEET		
DEBIT	CREDIT	DEBIT	CREDIT	DEBIT	CREDIT	
						1
						2
						3
						4
						5
						6
						7
						8
						9
						10
						11
						12
						13
						14
						15
						16
						17
						18
						19

2.

APPENDIX: DEPRECIATION METHODS

Exercise 5Apx-1A

Straight-Line Depreciation

Year	Depreciable Cost	×	Rate	=	Depreciation Expense	Accumulated Depreciation End of Year	Book Value End of Year

Exercise 5Apx-2A

Sum-of-the-Years'-Digits

Year	Depreciable Cost	×	Rate	=	Depreciation Expense	Accumulated Depreciation End of Year	Book Value End of Year

Exercise 5Apx-3A

Double-Declining-Balance Method

Year	Book Value Beginning of Year	×	Rate	=	Depreciation Expense	Accumulated Depreciation End of Year	Book Value End of Year

Name ______________________________

Exercise 5Apx-4A

Modified Accelerated Cost Recovery System

Year	Cost	×	Rate	=	Depreciation Expense	Accumulated Depreciation End of Year	Book Value End of Year

Exercise 5Apx-1B

Straight-Line Depreciation

Year	Depreciable Cost	×	Rate	=	Depreciation Expense	Accumulated Depreciation End of Year	Book Value End of Year

Exercise 5Apx-2B

Sum-of-the-Years'-Digits

Year	Depreciable Cost	×	Rate	=	Depreciation Expense	Accumulated Depreciation End of Year	Book Value End of Year

Exercise 5Apx-3B

Double-Declining-Balance Method

Year	Book Value Beginning of Year	×	Rate	=	Depreciation Expense	Accumulated Depreciation End of Year	Book Value End of Year

Exercise 5Apx-4B

Modified Accelerated Cost Recovery System

Year	Cost	×	Rate	=	Depreciation Expense	Accumulated Depreciation End of Year	Book Value End of Year

Exercise 6-1A

Exercise 6-2A

Exercise 6-3A

Name ______________________________

Exercise 6-4A

GENERAL JOURNAL

PAGE 1

	DATE		DESCRIPTION	POST. REF.	DEBIT	CREDIT	
1							1
2							2
3							3
4							4
5							5
6							6
7							7
8							8
9							9
10							10
11							11
12							12
13							13
14							14
15							15
16							16
17							17
18							18
19							19
20							20
21							21
22							22
23							23

Exercise 6-4A (Concluded)

Name ______________________________

Exercise 6-5A

GENERAL JOURNAL

PAGE

	DATE		DESCRIPTION	POST. REF.	DEBIT	CREDIT	
1							1
2							2
3							3
4							4
5							5
6							6
7							7
8							8
9							9
10							10
11							11
12							12
13							13
14							14
15							15
16							16
17							17
18							18
19							19
20							20
21							21
22							22
23							23
24							24
25							25
26							26
27							27
28							28
29							29
30							30
31							31
32							32
33							33
34							34
35							35
36							36

Exercise 6-5A (Concluded)

Cash 101

Bal.	500		

Accounts Receivable 122

Bal.	1,500		

Wages Payable 219

		Bal.	400

Chris Williams, Capital 311

		Bal.	9,000

Chris Williams, Drawing 312

Bal.	1,000		

Income Summary 313

Golf Instruction Fees 401

		Bal.	4,000

Wages Expense 511

Bal.	800		

Advertising Expense 512

Bal.	200		

Travel Expense 515

Bal.	600		

Supplies Expense 524

Bal.	500		

Insurance Expense 535

Bal.	100		

Postage Expense 536

Bal.	50		

Gas and Oil Expense 538

Bal.	150		

Miscellaneous Expense 549

Bal.	80		

Name ________________________________

Exercise 6-6A

GENERAL JOURNAL

PAGE

DATE		DESCRIPTION	POST. REF.	DEBIT	CREDIT

Exercise 6-6A (Concluded)

Accum. Depr.—Delivery Equip. 185.1

		Bal.	100

Wages Payable 219

		Bal.	200

Saburo Goto, Capital 311

		Bal.	4,000

Saburo Goto, Drawing 312

Bal.	800		

Income Summary 313

Delivery Fees 401

		Bal.	2,200

Wages Expense 511

Bal.	1,800		

Advertising Expense 512

Bal.	80		

Rent Expense 521

Bal.	500		

Supplies Expense 523

Bal.	120		

Telephone Expense 525

Bal.	58		

Electricity Expense 533

Bal.	44		

Insurance Expense 535

Bal.	30		

Gas and Oil Expense 538

Bal.	38		

Depr. Exp.—Delivery Equip. 541

Bal.	100		

Miscellaneous Expense 549

Bal.	33		

Problem 6-7A

1.

2.

Problem 6-7A (Concluded)

3.

Name ____________________

Problem 6-8A

1.

GENERAL JOURNAL

PAGE 10

	DATE		DESCRIPTION	POST. REF.	DEBIT	CREDIT	
1							1
2							2
3							3
4							4
5							5
6							6
7							7
8							8
9							9
10							10
11							11
12							12
13							13
14							14
15							15
16							16
17							17
18							18

Problem 6-8A (Continued)

2.

GENERAL JOURNAL

PAGE 11

	DATE		DESCRIPTION	POST. REF.	DEBIT	CREDIT	
1							1
2							2
3							3
4							4
5							5
6							6
7							7
8							8
9							9
10							10
11							11
12							12
13							13
14							14
15							15
16							16
17							17
18							18
19							19
20							20
21							21
22							22
23							23

1. and 2.

GENERAL LEDGER

ACCOUNT Cash ACCOUNT NO. 101

DATE		ITEM	POST. REF.	DEBIT	CREDIT	BALANCE DEBIT	BALANCE CREDIT
20-- Jan.	31	Balance	✓			3 6 7 3 00	

Problem 6-8A (Continued)

ACCOUNT Accounts Receivable ACCOUNT NO. 122

DATE		ITEM	POST. REF.	DEBIT	CREDIT	BALANCE DEBIT	BALANCE CREDIT
20-- Jan.	31	Balance	✓			1,450 00	

ACCOUNT Supplies ACCOUNT NO. 141

DATE		ITEM	POST. REF.	DEBIT	CREDIT	BALANCE DEBIT	BALANCE CREDIT
20-- Jan.	31	Balance	✓			700 00	

ACCOUNT Prepaid Insurance ACCOUNT NO. 145

DATE		ITEM	POST. REF.	DEBIT	CREDIT	BALANCE DEBIT	BALANCE CREDIT
20-- Jan.	31	Balance	✓			900 00	

ACCOUNT Delivery Equipment ACCOUNT NO. 185

DATE		ITEM	POST. REF.	DEBIT	CREDIT	BALANCE DEBIT	BALANCE CREDIT
20-- Jan.	31	Balance	✓			3,200 00	

ACCOUNT Accumulated Depreciation—Delivery Equipment ACCOUNT NO. 185.1

DATE		ITEM	POST. REF.	DEBIT	CREDIT	BALANCE DEBIT	BALANCE CREDIT

Problem 6-8A (Continued)

ACCOUNT Accounts Payable — ACCOUNT NO. 202

DATE		ITEM	POST. REF.	DEBIT	CREDIT	BALANCE DEBIT	BALANCE CREDIT
20-- Jan.	31	Balance	✓				12,000 00

ACCOUNT Wages Payable — ACCOUNT NO. 219

DATE		ITEM	POST. REF.	DEBIT	CREDIT	BALANCE DEBIT	BALANCE CREDIT

ACCOUNT Don Megaffin, Capital — ACCOUNT NO. 311

DATE		ITEM	POST. REF.	DEBIT	CREDIT	BALANCE DEBIT	BALANCE CREDIT
20-- Jan.	31	Balance	✓				8,000 00

ACCOUNT Don Megaffin, Drawing — ACCOUNT NO. 312

DATE		ITEM	POST. REF.	DEBIT	CREDIT	BALANCE DEBIT	BALANCE CREDIT
20-- Jan.	31	Balance	✓			1,100 00	

ACCOUNT Income Summary — ACCOUNT NO. 313

DATE		ITEM	POST. REF.	DEBIT	CREDIT	BALANCE DEBIT	BALANCE CREDIT

Name ______________________________

Problem 6-8A (Continued)

ACCOUNT Repair Fees ACCOUNT NO. 401

DATE		ITEM	POST. REF.	DEBIT	CREDIT	BALANCE DEBIT	BALANCE CREDIT
20-- Jan.	31	Balance	✓				4,700.00

ACCOUNT Wages Expense ACCOUNT NO. 511

DATE		ITEM	POST. REF.	DEBIT	CREDIT	BALANCE DEBIT	BALANCE CREDIT
20-- Jan.	31	Balance	✓			1,750.00	

ACCOUNT Advertising Expense ACCOUNT NO. 512

DATE		ITEM	POST. REF.	DEBIT	CREDIT	BALANCE DEBIT	BALANCE CREDIT
20-- Jan.	31	Balance	✓			200.00	

ACCOUNT Rent Expense ACCOUNT NO. 521

DATE		ITEM	POST. REF.	DEBIT	CREDIT	BALANCE DEBIT	BALANCE CREDIT
20-- Jan.	31	Balance	✓			640.00	

ACCOUNT Supplies Expense ACCOUNT NO. 523

DATE		ITEM	POST. REF.	DEBIT	CREDIT	BALANCE DEBIT	BALANCE CREDIT

Problem 6-8A (Continued)

ACCOUNT Telephone Expense ACCOUNT NO. 525

DATE		ITEM	POST. REF.	DEBIT	CREDIT	BALANCE DEBIT	BALANCE CREDIT
20-- Jan.	31	Balance	✓			50 00	

ACCOUNT Insurance Expense ACCOUNT NO. 535

DATE		ITEM	POST. REF.	DEBIT	CREDIT	BALANCE DEBIT	BALANCE CREDIT

ACCOUNT Gas and Oil Expense ACCOUNT NO. 538

DATE		ITEM	POST. REF.	DEBIT	CREDIT	BALANCE DEBIT	BALANCE CREDIT
20-- Jan.	31	Balance	✓			200 00	

ACCOUNT Depreciation Expense—Delivery Equipment ACCOUNT NO. 541

DATE		ITEM	POST. REF.	DEBIT	CREDIT	BALANCE DEBIT	BALANCE CREDIT

ACCOUNT Miscellaneous Expense ACCOUNT NO. 549

DATE		ITEM	POST. REF.	DEBIT	CREDIT	BALANCE DEBIT	BALANCE CREDIT
20-- Jan.	31	Balance	✓			37 00	

Problem 6-8A (Concluded)

3.

ACCOUNT TITLE	ACCT. NO.	DEBIT BALANCE	CREDIT BALANCE

Problem 6-9A

Exercise 6-1B

Exercise 6-2B

Name ______________________________

Exercise 6-3B

Exercise 6-4B

GENERAL JOURNAL

PAGE 1

DATE		DESCRIPTION	POST. REF.	DEBIT	CREDIT

Name ______________________________

Exercise 6-4B (Concluded)

Exercise 6-5B

GENERAL JOURNAL

PAGE

	DATE		DESCRIPTION	POST. REF.	DEBIT	CREDIT	
1							1
2							2
3							3
4							4
5							5
6							6
7							7
8							8
9							9
10							10
11							11
12							12
13							13
14							14
15							15
16							16
17							17
18							18
19							19
20							20
21							21
22							22
23							23
24							24
25							25
26							26
27							27
28							28
29							29
30							30
31							31
32							32
33							33
34							34
35							35
36							36

Exercise 6-5B (Concluded)

Cash 101

Bal.	600		

Accounts Receivable 122

Bal.	1,800		

Wages Payable 219

		Bal.	500

Mark Thrasher, Capital 311

		Bal.	8,000

Mark Thrasher, Drawing 312

Bal.	800		

Income Summary 313

Lawn Service Fees 401

		Bal.	5,000

Wages Expense 511

Bal.	400		

Advertising Expense 512

Bal.	600		

Travel Expense 515

Bal.	100		

Supplies Expense 524

Bal.	900		

Insurance Expense 535

Bal.	300		

Postage Expense 536

Bal.	40		

Gas and Oil Expense 538

Bal.	700		

Miscellaneous Expense 549

Bal.	200		

Exercise 6-6B

GENERAL JOURNAL

PAGE

DATE	DESCRIPTION	POST. REF.	DEBIT	CREDIT

Exercise 6-6B (Concluded)

Accum. Depr.—Office Equip. 181.1			
		Bal.	110

Wages Payable 219			
		Bal.	260

Raquel Zapata, Capital 311			
		Bal.	6,000

Raquel Zapata, Drawing 312			
Bal.	2,000		

Income Summary 313	

Referral Fees 401			
		Bal.	2,813

Wages Expense 511		
Bal.	1,080	

Advertising Expense 512		
Bal.	34	

Rent Expense 521		
Bal.	900	

Supplies Expense 523		
Bal.	322	

Telephone Expense 525		
Bal.	133	

Utilities Expense 533		
Bal.	102	

Insurance Expense 535		
Bal.	120	

Gas and Oil Expense 538		
Bal.	88	

Depr. Exp.—Office Equip. 541		
Bal.	110	

Miscellaneous Expense 549		
Bal.	98	

Problem 6-7B

1.

2.

Problem 6-7B (Concluded)

3.

Problem 6-8B

1.

GENERAL JOURNAL

PAGE 10

	DATE		DESCRIPTION	POST. REF.	DEBIT	CREDIT	
1							1
2							2
3							3
4							4
5							5
6							6
7							7
8							8
9							9
10							10
11							11
12							12
13							13
14							14
15							15
16							16
17							17
18							18

Problem 6-8B (Continued)

2.

GENERAL JOURNAL

PAGE 11

DATE		DESCRIPTION	POST. REF.	DEBIT	CREDIT

1. and 2.

GENERAL LEDGER

ACCOUNT Cash ACCOUNT NO. 101

DATE		ITEM	POST. REF.	DEBIT	CREDIT	BALANCE DEBIT	BALANCE CREDIT
20-- June	30	Balance	✓			5285 00	

Problem 6-8B (Continued)

ACCOUNT Accounts Receivable ACCOUNT NO. 122

DATE		ITEM	POST. REF.	DEBIT	CREDIT	BALANCE DEBIT	BALANCE CREDIT
20-- June	30	Balance	✓			1,075 00	

ACCOUNT Supplies ACCOUNT NO. 141

DATE		ITEM	POST. REF.	DEBIT	CREDIT	BALANCE DEBIT	BALANCE CREDIT
20-- June	30	Balance	✓			750 00	

ACCOUNT Prepaid Insurance ACCOUNT NO. 145

DATE		ITEM	POST. REF.	DEBIT	CREDIT	BALANCE DEBIT	BALANCE CREDIT
20-- June	30	Balance	✓			500 00	

ACCOUNT Office Equipment ACCOUNT NO. 181

DATE		ITEM	POST. REF.	DEBIT	CREDIT	BALANCE DEBIT	BALANCE CREDIT
20-- June	30	Balance	✓			2,200 00	

ACCOUNT Accumulated Depreciation—Office Equipment ACCOUNT NO. 181.1

DATE		ITEM	POST. REF.	DEBIT	CREDIT	BALANCE DEBIT	BALANCE CREDIT

Name ______________________________

Problem 6-8B (Continued)

ACCOUNT Accounts Payable ACCOUNT NO. 202

DATE		ITEM	POST. REF.	DEBIT	CREDIT	BALANCE DEBIT	BALANCE CREDIT
20-- June	30	Balance	✓				1,500.00

ACCOUNT Wages Payable ACCOUNT NO. 219

DATE		ITEM	POST. REF.	DEBIT	CREDIT	BALANCE DEBIT	BALANCE CREDIT

ACCOUNT Juanita Alvarez, Capital ACCOUNT NO. 311

DATE		ITEM	POST. REF.	DEBIT	CREDIT	BALANCE DEBIT	BALANCE CREDIT
20-- June	30	Balance	✓				7,000.00

ACCOUNT Juanita Alvarez, Drawing ACCOUNT NO. 312

DATE		ITEM	POST. REF.	DEBIT	CREDIT	BALANCE DEBIT	BALANCE CREDIT
20-- June	30	Balance	✓			800.00	

ACCOUNT Income Summary ACCOUNT NO. 313

DATE		ITEM	POST. REF.	DEBIT	CREDIT	BALANCE DEBIT	BALANCE CREDIT

Problem 6-8B (Continued)

ACCOUNT Consulting Fees ACCOUNT NO. 401

DATE		ITEM	POST. REF.	DEBIT	CREDIT	BALANCE DEBIT	BALANCE CREDIT
20-- June	30	Balance	✓				4,204.00

ACCOUNT Wages Expense ACCOUNT NO. 511

DATE		ITEM	POST. REF.	DEBIT	CREDIT	BALANCE DEBIT	BALANCE CREDIT
20-- June	30	Balance	✓			1,400.00	

ACCOUNT Advertising Expense ACCOUNT NO. 512

DATE		ITEM	POST. REF.	DEBIT	CREDIT	BALANCE DEBIT	BALANCE CREDIT
20-- June	30	Balance	✓			60.00	

ACCOUNT Rent Expense ACCOUNT NO. 521

DATE		ITEM	POST. REF.	DEBIT	CREDIT	BALANCE DEBIT	BALANCE CREDIT
20-- June	30	Balance	✓			500.00	

ACCOUNT Supplies Expense ACCOUNT NO. 523

DATE		ITEM	POST. REF.	DEBIT	CREDIT	BALANCE DEBIT	BALANCE CREDIT

Problem 6-8B (Continued)

ACCOUNT Telephone Expense ACCOUNT NO. 525

DATE		ITEM	POST. REF.	DEBIT	CREDIT	BALANCE DEBIT	BALANCE CREDIT
20-- June	30	Balance	✓			46 00	

ACCOUNT Electricity Expense ACCOUNT NO. 533

DATE		ITEM	POST. REF.	DEBIT	CREDIT	BALANCE DEBIT	BALANCE CREDIT
20-- June	30	Balance	✓			39 00	

ACCOUNT Insurance Expense ACCOUNT NO. 535

DATE		ITEM	POST. REF.	DEBIT	CREDIT	BALANCE DEBIT	BALANCE CREDIT

ACCOUNT Gas and Oil Expense ACCOUNT NO. 538

DATE		ITEM	POST. REF.	DEBIT	CREDIT	BALANCE DEBIT	BALANCE CREDIT
20-- June	30	Balance	✓			28 00	

ACCOUNT Depreciation Expense—Office Equipment ACCOUNT NO. 541

DATE		ITEM	POST. REF.	DEBIT	CREDIT	BALANCE DEBIT	BALANCE CREDIT

Problem 6-8B (Concluded)

ACCOUNT Miscellaneous Expense ACCOUNT NO. 549

DATE		ITEM	POST. REF.	DEBIT	CREDIT	BALANCE DEBIT	BALANCE CREDIT
20-- June	30	Balance	✓			21 00	

3.

ACCOUNT TITLE	ACCT. NO.	DEBIT BALANCE	CREDIT BALANCE

Name ______________________________

Problem 6-9B

Mastery Problem

GENERAL JOURNAL

PAGE 4

DATE		DESCRIPTION	POST. REF.	DEBIT	CREDIT

Mastery Problem (Continued)

Mastery Problem (Concluded)

Name ____________________

Challenge Problem

Challenge Problem (Concluded)

Name ______________________________

Exercise 6Apx-1A

a. ____________________

b. ____________________

c. ____________________

d. ____________________

e. ____________________

f. ____________________

g. ____________________

h. ____________________

i. ____________________

j. ____________________

k. ____________________

Problem 6Apx-2A

Exercise 6Apx-1B

a. ____________________

b. ____________________

c. ____________________

d. ____________________

e. ____________________

f. ____________________

g. ____________________

h. ____________________

i. ____________________

j. ____________________

k. ____________________

Problem 6Apx-2B

Name ______________________________

Comprehensive Problem 1: The Accounting Cycle

1.

GENERAL JOURNAL

PAGE 1

DATE		DESCRIPTION	POST. REF.	DEBIT	CREDIT

Comprehensive Problem 1 (Continued)

GENERAL JOURNAL

PAGE 2

DATE		DESCRIPTION	POST. REF.	DEBIT	CREDIT

Name ______________________________

Comprehensive Problem 1 (Continued)

GENERAL JOURNAL

PAGE 3

	DATE		DESCRIPTION	POST. REF.	DEBIT	CREDIT	
1							1
2							2
3							3
4							4
5							5
6							6
7							7
8							8
9							9
10							10
11							11
12							12
13							13
14							14
15							15
16							16
17							17
18							18
19							19
20							20
21							21
22							22
23							23
24							24
25							25
26							26
27							27
28							28
29							29
30							30
31							31
32							32
33							33
34							34
35							35

Comprehensive Problem 1 (Continued)

GENERAL JOURNAL

PAGE 4

	DATE		DESCRIPTION	POST. REF.	DEBIT	CREDIT	
1							1
2							2
3							3
4							4
5							5
6							6
7							7
8							8
9							9
10							10
11							11

2., 6., and 11.

GENERAL LEDGER

ACCOUNT Cash ACCOUNT NO. 101

DATE		ITEM	POST. REF.	DEBIT	CREDIT	BALANCE	
						DEBIT	CREDIT

Name ______________________________

Comprehensive Problem 1 (Continued)

ACCOUNT Office Supplies ACCOUNT NO. 142

DATE		ITEM	POST. REF.	DEBIT	CREDIT	BALANCE DEBIT	BALANCE CREDIT

ACCOUNT Food Supplies ACCOUNT NO. 144

DATE		ITEM	POST. REF.	DEBIT	CREDIT	BALANCE DEBIT	BALANCE CREDIT

ACCOUNT Prepaid Insurance ACCOUNT NO. 145

DATE		ITEM	POST. REF.	DEBIT	CREDIT	BALANCE DEBIT	BALANCE CREDIT

ACCOUNT Fishing Boats ACCOUNT NO. 181

DATE		ITEM	POST. REF.	DEBIT	CREDIT	BALANCE DEBIT	BALANCE CREDIT

Comprehensive Problem 1 (Continued)

ACCOUNT Accumulated Depreciation—Fishing Boats ACCOUNT NO. 181.1

DATE		ITEM	POST. REF.	DEBIT	CREDIT	BALANCE DEBIT	BALANCE CREDIT

ACCOUNT Accounts Payable ACCOUNT NO. 202

DATE		ITEM	POST. REF.	DEBIT	CREDIT	BALANCE DEBIT	BALANCE CREDIT

ACCOUNT Wages Payable ACCOUNT NO. 219

DATE		ITEM	POST. REF.	DEBIT	CREDIT	BALANCE DEBIT	BALANCE CREDIT

ACCOUNT Bob Night, Capital ACCOUNT NO. 311

DATE		ITEM	POST. REF.	DEBIT	CREDIT	BALANCE DEBIT	BALANCE CREDIT

Comprehensive Problem 1 (Continued)

ACCOUNT Bob Night, Drawing ACCOUNT NO. 312

DATE		ITEM	POST. REF.	DEBIT	CREDIT	BALANCE DEBIT	BALANCE CREDIT

ACCOUNT Income Summary ACCOUNT NO. 313

DATE		ITEM	POST. REF.	DEBIT	CREDIT	BALANCE DEBIT	BALANCE CREDIT

ACCOUNT Registration Fees ACCOUNT NO. 401

DATE		ITEM	POST. REF.	DEBIT	CREDIT	BALANCE DEBIT	BALANCE CREDIT

Comprehensive Problem 1 (Continued)

ACCOUNT Wages Expense ACCOUNT NO. 511

DATE		ITEM	POST. REF.	DEBIT	CREDIT	BALANCE DEBIT	BALANCE CREDIT

ACCOUNT Rent Expense ACCOUNT NO. 521

DATE		ITEM	POST. REF.	DEBIT	CREDIT	BALANCE DEBIT	BALANCE CREDIT

ACCOUNT Office Supplies Expense ACCOUNT NO. 523

DATE		ITEM	POST. REF.	DEBIT	CREDIT	BALANCE DEBIT	BALANCE CREDIT

ACCOUNT Food Supplies Expense ACCOUNT NO. 524

DATE		ITEM	POST. REF.	DEBIT	CREDIT	BALANCE DEBIT	BALANCE CREDIT

Name ______________________________

Comprehensive Problem 1 (Continued)

ACCOUNT Telephone Expense ACCOUNT NO. 525

DATE		ITEM	POST. REF.	DEBIT	CREDIT	BALANCE DEBIT	BALANCE CREDIT

ACCOUNT Utilities Expense ACCOUNT NO. 533

DATE		ITEM	POST. REF.	DEBIT	CREDIT	BALANCE DEBIT	BALANCE CREDIT

ACCOUNT Insurance Expense ACCOUNT NO. 535

DATE		ITEM	POST. REF.	DEBIT	CREDIT	BALANCE DEBIT	BALANCE CREDIT

ACCOUNT Postage Expense ACCOUNT NO. 536

DATE		ITEM	POST. REF.	DEBIT	CREDIT	BALANCE DEBIT	BALANCE CREDIT

ACCOUNT Depreciation Expense—Fishing Boats ACCOUNT NO. 542

DATE		ITEM	POST. REF.	DEBIT	CREDIT	BALANCE DEBIT	BALANCE CREDIT

Comprehensive Problem 1 (Continued)

3. and 4.

	ACCOUNT TITLE	TRIAL BALANCE		ADJUSTMENTS	
		DEBIT	CREDIT	DEBIT	CREDIT
1					
2					
3					
4					
5					
6					
7					
8					
9					
10					
11					
12					
13					
14					
15					
16					
17					
18					
19					
20					
21					
22					
23					
24					
25					
26					
27					
28					
29					
30					
31					

Comprehensive Problem 1 (Continued)

ADJUSTED TRIAL BALANCE		INCOME STATEMENT		BALANCE SHEET		
DEBIT	CREDIT	DEBIT	CREDIT	DEBIT	CREDIT	
						1
						2
						3
						4
						5
						6
						7
						8
						9
						10
						11
						12
						13
						14
						15
						16
						17
						18
						19
						20
						21
						22
						23
						24
						25
						26
						27
						28
						29
						30
						31

Comprehensive Problem 1 (Continued)

7.

8.

Name ______________________________

Comprehensive Problem 1 (Continued)

9.

Comprehensive Problem 1 (Continued)

5. and 10.

GENERAL JOURNAL

PAGE 5

	DATE		DESCRIPTION	POST. REF.	DEBIT	CREDIT	
1							1
2							2
3							3
4							4
5							5
6							6
7							7
8							8
9							9
10							10
11							11
12							12
13							13
14							14
15							15
16							16
17							17
18							18
19							19
20							20
21							21
22							22
23							23
24							24
25							25
26							26
27							27
28							28
29							29
30							30
31							31
32							32
33							33
34							34
35							35

Comprehensive Problem 1 (Concluded)

GENERAL JOURNAL

PAGE 6

	DATE		DESCRIPTION	POST. REF.	DEBIT	CREDIT	
1							1
2							2
3							3
4							4
5							5
6							6
7							7
8							8
9							9

12.

____

____

____

ACCOUNT	ACCT. NO.	DEBIT BALANCE	CREDIT BALANCE

Name ____________________

Comprehensive Problem 1, Period 2: The Accounting Cycle

1.

GENERAL JOURNAL

PAGE 5

	DATE		DESCRIPTION	POST. REF.	DEBIT	CREDIT	
1							1
2							2
3							3
4							4
5							5
6							6
7							7
8							8
9							9
10							10
11							11
12							12
13							13
14							14
15							15
16							16
17							17
18							18
19							19
20							20
21							21
22							22
23							23
24							24
25							25
26							26
27							27
28							28
29							29
30							30
31							31
32							32
33							33
34							34
35							35

Comprehensive Problem 1, Period 2 (Continued)

GENERAL JOURNAL

PAGE 6

DATE		DESCRIPTION	POST. REF.	DEBIT	CREDIT

Name ______________________________

Comprehensive Problem 1, Period 2 (Continued)

GENERAL JOURNAL

PAGE 7

DATE		DESCRIPTION	POST. REF.	DEBIT	CREDIT

Comprehensive Problem 1, Period 2 (Continued)

2., 6., and 11.

GENERAL LEDGER

ACCOUNT Cash ACCOUNT NO. 101

DATE		ITEM	POST. REF.	DEBIT	CREDIT	BALANCE DEBIT	BALANCE CREDIT
20-- Apr.	30	Balance	✓			130,650.00	

ACCOUNT Accounts Receivable ACCOUNT NO. 122

DATE		ITEM	POST. REF.	DEBIT	CREDIT	BALANCE DEBIT	BALANCE CREDIT

Name ______________________________

Comprehensive Problem 1, Period 2 (Continued)

ACCOUNT Office Supplies ACCOUNT NO. 142

DATE		ITEM	POST. REF.	DEBIT	CREDIT	BALANCE DEBIT	BALANCE CREDIT
20-- Apr.	30	Balance	✓			1 0 0 00	

ACCOUNT Food Supplies ACCOUNT NO. 144

DATE		ITEM	POST. REF.	DEBIT	CREDIT	BALANCE DEBIT	BALANCE CREDIT
20-- Apr.	30	Balance	✓			8 0 0 0 00	

ACCOUNT Prepaid Insurance ACCOUNT NO. 145

DATE		ITEM	POST. REF.	DEBIT	CREDIT	BALANCE DEBIT	BALANCE CREDIT
20-- Apr.	30	Balance	✓			7 5 0 0 00	

ACCOUNT Prepaid Subscriptions ACCOUNT NO. 146

DATE		ITEM	POST. REF.	DEBIT	CREDIT	BALANCE DEBIT	BALANCE CREDIT

Comprehensive Problem 1, Period 2 (Continued)

ACCOUNT Land ACCOUNT NO. 161

DATE		ITEM	POST. REF.	DEBIT	CREDIT	BALANCE DEBIT	BALANCE CREDIT

ACCOUNT Buildings ACCOUNT NO. 171

DATE		ITEM	POST. REF.	DEBIT	CREDIT	BALANCE DEBIT	BALANCE CREDIT

ACCOUNT Accumulated Depreciation—Buildings ACCOUNT NO. 171.1

DATE		ITEM	POST. REF.	DEBIT	CREDIT	BALANCE DEBIT	BALANCE CREDIT

ACCOUNT Fishing Boats ACCOUNT NO. 181

DATE		ITEM	POST. REF.	DEBIT	CREDIT	BALANCE DEBIT	BALANCE CREDIT
20-- Apr.	30	Balance	✓			60 0 0 0 00	

Comprehensive Problem 1, Period 2 (Continued)

ACCOUNT Accumulated Depreciation—Fishing Boats ACCOUNT NO. 181.1

DATE		ITEM	POST. REF.	DEBIT	CREDIT	BALANCE DEBIT	BALANCE CREDIT
20-- Apr.	30	Balance	✓				1,000 00

ACCOUNT Surround Sound System ACCOUNT NO. 182

DATE		ITEM	POST. REF.	DEBIT	CREDIT	BALANCE DEBIT	BALANCE CREDIT

ACCOUNT Accumulated Depreciation—Surround Sound System ACCOUNT NO. 182.1

DATE		ITEM	POST. REF.	DEBIT	CREDIT	BALANCE DEBIT	BALANCE CREDIT

ACCOUNT Big Screen TV ACCOUNT NO. 183

DATE		ITEM	POST. REF.	DEBIT	CREDIT	BALANCE DEBIT	BALANCE CREDIT

ACCOUNT Accumulated Depreciation—Big Screen TV ACCOUNT NO. 183.1

DATE		ITEM	POST. REF.	DEBIT	CREDIT	BALANCE DEBIT	BALANCE CREDIT

Comprehensive Problem 1, Period 2 (Continued)

ACCOUNT Accounts Payable ACCOUNT NO. 202

DATE		ITEM	POST. REF.	DEBIT	CREDIT	BALANCE DEBIT	BALANCE CREDIT
20-- Apr.	30	Balance	✓				66,500.00

ACCOUNT Wages Payable ACCOUNT NO. 219

DATE		ITEM	POST. REF.	DEBIT	CREDIT	BALANCE DEBIT	BALANCE CREDIT
20-- Apr.	30	Balance	✓				500.00

ACCOUNT Bob Night, Capital ACCOUNT NO. 311

DATE		ITEM	POST. REF.	DEBIT	CREDIT	BALANCE DEBIT	BALANCE CREDIT
20-- Apr.	30	Balance	✓				138,250.00

ACCOUNT Bob Night, Drawing ACCOUNT NO. 312

DATE		ITEM	POST. REF.	DEBIT	CREDIT	BALANCE DEBIT	BALANCE CREDIT

Comprehensive Problem 1, Period 2 (Continued)

ACCOUNT Income Summary ACCOUNT NO. 313

DATE	ITEM	POST. REF.	DEBIT	CREDIT	BALANCE DEBIT	BALANCE CREDIT

ACCOUNT Registration Fees ACCOUNT NO. 401

DATE	ITEM	POST. REF.	DEBIT	CREDIT	BALANCE DEBIT	BALANCE CREDIT

ACCOUNT Vending Commission Revenue ACCOUNT NO. 404

DATE	ITEM	POST. REF.	DEBIT	CREDIT	BALANCE DEBIT	BALANCE CREDIT

ACCOUNT Wages Expense ACCOUNT NO. 511

DATE	ITEM	POST. REF.	DEBIT	CREDIT	BALANCE DEBIT	BALANCE CREDIT

Comprehensive Problem 1, Period 2 (Continued)

ACCOUNT Advertising Expense ACCOUNT NO. 512

DATE		ITEM	POST. REF.	DEBIT	CREDIT	BALANCE DEBIT	BALANCE CREDIT

ACCOUNT Rent Expense ACCOUNT NO. 521

DATE		ITEM	POST. REF.	DEBIT	CREDIT	BALANCE DEBIT	BALANCE CREDIT

ACCOUNT Office Supplies Expense ACCOUNT NO. 523

DATE		ITEM	POST. REF.	DEBIT	CREDIT	BALANCE DEBIT	BALANCE CREDIT

ACCOUNT Food Supplies Expense ACCOUNT NO. 524

DATE		ITEM	POST. REF.	DEBIT	CREDIT	BALANCE DEBIT	BALANCE CREDIT

Comprehensive Problem 1, Period 2 (Continued)

ACCOUNT Telephone Expense ACCOUNT NO. 525

DATE		ITEM	POST. REF.	DEBIT	CREDIT	BALANCE DEBIT	BALANCE CREDIT

ACCOUNT Utilities Expense ACCOUNT NO. 533

DATE		ITEM	POST. REF.	DEBIT	CREDIT	BALANCE DEBIT	BALANCE CREDIT

ACCOUNT Insurance Expense ACCOUNT NO. 535

DATE		ITEM	POST. REF.	DEBIT	CREDIT	BALANCE DEBIT	BALANCE CREDIT

ACCOUNT Postage Expense ACCOUNT NO. 536

DATE		ITEM	POST. REF.	DEBIT	CREDIT	BALANCE DEBIT	BALANCE CREDIT

Comprehensive Problem 1, Period 2 (Continued)

ACCOUNT Repair Expense ACCOUNT NO. 537

DATE		ITEM	POST. REF.	DEBIT	CREDIT	BALANCE DEBIT	BALANCE CREDIT

ACCOUNT Depreciation Expense—Buildings ACCOUNT NO. 540

DATE		ITEM	POST. REF.	DEBIT	CREDIT	BALANCE DEBIT	BALANCE CREDIT

ACCOUNT Depreciation Expense—Surround Sound System ACCOUNT NO. 541

DATE		ITEM	POST. REF.	DEBIT	CREDIT	BALANCE DEBIT	BALANCE CREDIT

ACCOUNT Depreciation Expense—Fishing Boats ACCOUNT NO. 542

DATE		ITEM	POST. REF.	DEBIT	CREDIT	BALANCE DEBIT	BALANCE CREDIT

Comprehensive Problem 1, Period 2 (Continued)

ACCOUNT Depreciation Expense—Big Screen TV ACCOUNT NO. 543

DATE	ITEM	POST. REF.	DEBIT	CREDIT	BALANCE DEBIT	BALANCE CREDIT

ACCOUNT Satellite Programming Expense ACCOUNT NO. 546

DATE	ITEM	POST. REF.	DEBIT	CREDIT	BALANCE DEBIT	BALANCE CREDIT

ACCOUNT Subscriptions Expense ACCOUNT NO. 548

DATE	ITEM	POST. REF.	DEBIT	CREDIT	BALANCE DEBIT	BALANCE CREDIT

Comprehensive Problem 1, Period 2 (Continued)
3. and 4.

	ACCOUNT TITLE	TRIAL BALANCE DEBIT	TRIAL BALANCE CREDIT	ADJUSTMENTS DEBIT	ADJUSTMENTS CREDIT
1					
2					
3					
4					
5					
6					
7					
8					
9					
10					
11					
12					
13					
14					
15					
16					
17					
18					
19					
20					
21					
22					
23					
24					
25					
26					
27					
28					
29					
30					
31					
32					
33					
34					
35					
36					
37					
38					
39					
40					

Comprehensive Problem 1, Period 2 (Continued)

ADJUSTED TRIAL BALANCE		INCOME STATEMENT		BALANCE SHEET		
DEBIT	CREDIT	DEBIT	CREDIT	DEBIT	CREDIT	
						1
						2
						3
						4
						5
						6
						7
						8
						9
						10
						11
						12
						13
						14
						15
						16
						17
						18
						19
						20
						21
						22
						23
						24
						25
						26
						27
						28
						29
						30
						31
						32
						33
						34
						35
						36
						37
						38
						39
						40

Comprehensive Problem 1, Period 2 (Continued)

5.

GENERAL JOURNAL

PAGE 8

	DATE		DESCRIPTION	POST. REF.	DEBIT	CREDIT	
1							1
2							2
3							3
4							4
5							5
6							6
7							7
8							8
9							9
10							10
11							11
12							12
13							13
14							14
15							15
16							16
17							17
18							18
19							19
20							20
21							21
22							22
23							23
24							24
25							25
26							26
27							27
28							28
29							29
30							30
31							31
32							32
33							33
34							34
35							35

Name ______________________

Comprehensive Problem 1, Period 2 (Continued)

7.

8.

Comprehensive Problem 1, Period 2 (Continued)

9.

Name ______________________________

Comprehensive Problem 1, Period 2 (Continued)

10.

GENERAL JOURNAL

PAGE 9

	DATE		DESCRIPTION	POST. REF.	DEBIT	CREDIT	
1							1
2							2
3							3
4							4
5							5
6							6
7							7
8							8
9							9
10							10
11							11
12							12
13							13
14							14
15							15
16							16
17							17
18							18
19							19
20							20
21							21
22							22
23							23
24							24
25							25
26							26
27							27
28							28
29							29
30							30
31							31
32							32
33							33
34							34
35							35

Comprehensive Problem 1, Period 2 (Concluded)

12.

ACCOUNT TITLE	ACCT. NO.	DEBIT BALANCE	CREDIT BALANCE

Name ______________________________

Exercise 7-1A

1. ____________________
2. ____________________
3. ____________________
4. ____________________
5. ____________________
6. ____________________
7. ____________________

Exercise 7-2A

DEPOSIT TICKET 63-1209/631

WIZARD BANK
3711 Buena Vista Dr.
Orlando, FL 32811-1314

Date______________________ 20____

CHECKS AND OTHER ITEMS ARE RECEIVED FOR DEPOSIT SUBJECT TO THE TERMS AND CONDITIONS OF THIS FINANCIAL INSTITUTION'S ACCOUNT AGREEMENT.

____
SIGN HERE ONLY IF CASH RECEIVED FROM DEPOSIT

CURRENCY		
COIN		
CHECKS		
TOTAL FROM OTHER SIDE		
SUBTOTAL		
LESS CASH RECEIVED		
NET DEPOSIT		

⑆063112094⑆ 0001632475⑈

Exercise 7-3A

No. 1

DATE ______________ 20____
TO ______________________
FOR ______________________

ACCT. ____________________

	DOLLARS	CENTS
BAL BRO'T FOR'D		
AMT. DEPOSITED		
TOTAL		
AMT. THIS CHECK		
BAL CAR'D FOR'D		

No. 1 63-1209/631

______________________ 20________

PAY TO THE ORDER OF ______________________________________ $ __________

____ Dollars

WIZARD BANK
3711 Buena Vista Dr.
Orlando, FL 32811-1314

FOR CLASSROOM USE ONLY

MEMO______________________ BY ______________________

⑆063112094⑆ 0001632475⑈

Exercise 7-4A

	Ending Bank Balance	Ending Check-book Balance
1.		
2.		
3.		
4.		
5.		
6.		
7.		

Exercise 7-5A

GENERAL JOURNAL PAGE

	DATE		DESCRIPTION	POST. REF.	DEBIT	CREDIT	
1							1
2							2
3							3
4							4
5							5
6							6
7							7
8							8
9							9
10							10
11							11
12							12
13							13
14							14
15							15
16							16
17							17
18							18
19							19
20							20
21							21

Name ________________________________

Exercise 7-6A

GENERAL JOURNAL

PAGE

	DATE		DESCRIPTION	POST. REF.	DEBIT	CREDIT	
1							1
2							2
3							3
4							4
5							5
6							6
7							7
8							8
9							9
10							10
11							11
12							12
13							13
14							14
15							15
16							16
17							17
18							18
19							19
20							20
21							21
22							22
23							23
24							24
25							25
26							26
27							27
28							28
29							29
30							30
31							31
32							32
33							33
34							34
35							35
36							36

Exercise 7-7A

GENERAL JOURNAL

PAGE

DATE		DESCRIPTION	POST. REF.	DEBIT	CREDIT

Name ______________________________

Problem 7-8A

1.

Problem 7-8A (Concluded)

2.

GENERAL JOURNAL

PAGE

DATE		DESCRIPTION	POST. REF.	DEBIT	CREDIT

Problem 7-9A

1.

Problem 7-9A (Concluded)

2.

GENERAL JOURNAL

PAGE

	DATE		DESCRIPTION	POST. REF.	DEBIT	CREDIT	
1							1
2							2
3							3
4							4
5							5
6							6
7							7
8							8
9							9
10							10
11							11
12							12
13							13
14							14
15							15
16							16
17							17
18							18
19							19

Name ________________________________

Problem 7-10A

1. and 3.

GENERAL JOURNAL

PAGE

	DATE		DESCRIPTION	POST. REF.	DEBIT	CREDIT	
1							1
2							2
3							3
4							4
5							5
6							6
7							7
8							8
9							9
10							10
11							11
12							12
13							13

Problem 7-10A (Concluded)

2. and 3.

PETTY CASH PAYMENTS FOR MONTH OF 20-- PAGE

					DISTRIBUTION OF PAYMENTS								
	DAY	DESCRIPTION	VOU. NO.	TOTAL AMOUNT	OFFICE SUPPLIES	POSTAGE EXPENSE	CHARIT. CONTRIB. EXPENSE	TELEPHONE EXPENSE	TRAVEL & ENTER. EXPENSE	MISC. EXPENSE	ACCOUNT	AMOUNT	
1													1
2													2
3													3
4													4
5													5
6													6
7													7
8													8
9													9
10													10
11													11
12													12
13													13
14													14
15													15
16													16
17													17
18													18
19													19
20													20
21													21
22													22

Problem 7-11A

1.

GENERAL JOURNAL PAGE 8

	DATE		DESCRIPTION	POST. REF.	DEBIT	CREDIT	
1							1
2							2
3							3
4							4
5							5
6							6
7							7
8							8
9							9
10							10
11							11
12							12
13							13
14							14
15							15
16							16
17							17
18							18
19							19
20							20
21							21
22							22
23							23

2.

ACCOUNT ______________________________ ACCOUNT NO. ________

DATE		ITEM	POST. REF.	DEBIT	CREDIT	BALANCE	
						DEBIT	CREDIT

3. The balance represents:

____

Exercise 7-1B

1. ____________________
2. ____________________
3. ____________________
4. ____________________
5. ____________________
6. ____________________
7. ____________________

Exercise 7-2B

63-1209
631

DEPOSIT TICKET

WIZARD BANK
3711 Buena Vista Dr.
Orlando, FL 32811-1314

Date______________________ 20____

CHECKS AND OTHER ITEMS ARE RECEIVED FOR DEPOSIT SUBJECT TO THE TERMS AND CONDITIONS OF THIS FINANCIAL INSTITUTION'S ACCOUNT AGREEMENT.

____
SIGN HERE ONLY IF CASH RECEIVED FROM DEPOSIT

CURRENCY			
COIN			
CHECKS			
TOTAL FROM OTHER SIDE			
SUBTOTAL			
LESS CASH RECEIVED			
NET DEPOSIT			

⑆063112094⑆ 0001632475⑈

Exercise 7-3B

No. 1

DATE ____________ 20____
TO ____________________
FOR ____________________

ACCT. ____________________

	DOLLARS	CENTS
BAL BRO'T FOR'D		
AMT. DEPOSITED		
TOTAL		
AMT. THIS CHECK		
BAL CAR'D FOR'D		

No. 1 63-1209/631

____________________ 20________

PAY TO THE ORDER OF____ $__________

____ Dollars

WIZARD BANK
3711 Buena Vista Dr.
Orlando, FL 32811-1314

FOR CLASSROOM USE ONLY

MEMO____________________ BY ____________________

⑆063112094⑆ 0001632475⑈

Name ______________________________

Exercise 7-4B

	Ending Bank Balance	Ending Checkbook Balance
1.		
2.		
3.		
4.		
5.		
6.		
7.		

Exercise 7-5B

GENERAL JOURNAL PAGE

	DATE		DESCRIPTION	POST. REF.	DEBIT	CREDIT	
1							1
2							2
3							3
4							4
5							5
6							6
7							7
8							8
9							9
10							10
11							11
12							12
13							13
14							14
15							15
16							16
17							17
18							18
19							19
20							20
21							21

Exercise 7-6B

GENERAL JOURNAL

PAGE

DATE		DESCRIPTION	POST. REF.	DEBIT	CREDIT

Name ______________________________

Exercise 7-7B

GENERAL JOURNAL

PAGE

	DATE		DESCRIPTION	POST. REF.	DEBIT	CREDIT	
1							1
2							2
3							3
4							4
5							5
6							6
7							7
8							8
9							9
10							10
11							11
12							12
13							13
14							14
15							15
16							16
17							17
18							18
19							19
20							20
21							21
22							22
23							23
24							24
25							25
26							26
27							27
28							28
29							29
30							30
31							31
32							32
33							33
34							34
35							35
36							36

Problem 7-8B

1.

Problem 7-8B (Concluded)

2.

GENERAL JOURNAL

PAGE

	DATE		DESCRIPTION	POST. REF.	DEBIT	CREDIT	
1							1
2							2
3							3
4							4
5							5
6							6
7							7
8							8
9							9
10							10
11							11
12							12
13							13
14							14
15							15

Problem 7-9B

1.

Problem 7-9B (Concluded)

2.

GENERAL JOURNAL

PAGE

	DATE		DESCRIPTION	POST. REF.	DEBIT	CREDIT	
1							1
2							2
3							3
4							4
5							5
6							6
7							7
8							8
9							9
10							10
11							11
12							12
13							13
14							14
15							15
16							16
17							17
18							18
19							19

Problem 7-10B

1. and 3.

GENERAL JOURNAL

PAGE

	DATE		DESCRIPTION	POST. REF.	DEBIT	CREDIT	
1							1
2							2
3							3
4							4
5							5
6							6
7							7
8							8
9							9
10							10
11							11
12							12
13							13

Problem 7-10B (Concluded)

2. and 3.

PETTY CASH PAYMENTS FOR MONTH OF 20-- PAGE

					DISTRIBUTION OF PAYMENTS								
	DAY	DESCRIPTION	VOU. NO.	TOTAL AMOUNT	OFFICE SUPPLIES	POSTAGE EXPENSE	CHARIT. CONTRIB. EXPENSE	TELEPHONE EXPENSE	TRAVEL & ENTER. EXPENSE	MISC. EXPENSE	ACCOUNT	AMOUNT	
1													1
2													2
3													3
4													4
5													5
6													6
7													7
8													8
9													9
10													10
11													11
12													12
13													13
14													14
15													15
16													16
17													17
18													18
19													19
20													20
21													21
22													22

Problem 7-11B

1.

GENERAL JOURNAL

PAGE 8

DATE		DESCRIPTION	POST. REF.	DEBIT	CREDIT

2.

ACCOUNT ACCOUNT NO.

DATE		ITEM	POST. REF.	DEBIT	CREDIT	BALANCE	
						DEBIT	CREDIT

3. The balance represents:

Mastery Problem

1.

PETTY CASH PAYMENTS FOR MONTH OF 20-- PAGE

	DAY	DESCRIPTION	VOU. NO.	TOTAL AMOUNT	DISTRIBUTION OF PAYMENTS								
					TRUCK EXPENSE	POSTAGE EXPENSE	CHARIT. CONTRIB. EXPENSE	TELEPHONE EXPENSE	ADVERT. EXPENSE.	MISC. EXPENSE	ACCOUNT	AMOUNT	
1													1
2													2
3													3
4													4
5													5
6													6
7													7
8													8
9													9
10													10
11													11
12													12
13													13
14													14
15													15
16													16
17													17
18													18
19													19
20													20
21													21
22													22

Mastery Problem (Continued)
2. and 3.

GENERAL JOURNAL

PAGE 1

DATE		DESCRIPTION	POST. REF.	DEBIT	CREDIT

Mastery Problem (Concluded)

GENERAL JOURNAL

PAGE 2

	DATE		DESCRIPTION	POST. REF.	DEBIT	CREDIT	
1							1
2							2
3							3
4							4
5							5
6							6
7							7
8							8
9							9
10							10
11							11
12							12
13							13
14							14

3.

Challenge Problem

1. Panera Bakery

GENERAL JOURNAL PAGE

DATE		DESCRIPTION	POST. REF.	DEBIT	CREDIT

Name ____________________

Challenge Problem (Concluded)

2. Lawrence Bank

GENERAL JOURNAL PAGE

DATE		DESCRIPTION	POST. REF.	DEBIT	CREDIT

APPENDIX: Internal Controls

Exercise 7Apx-1A

1. ____

____

2. ____

____

3. ____

____

4. ____

____

5. ____

____

Exercise 7Apx-2A

1. _____

2. _____

3. _____

4. _____

5. _____

Name ______________________________

Exercise 7Apx-3A

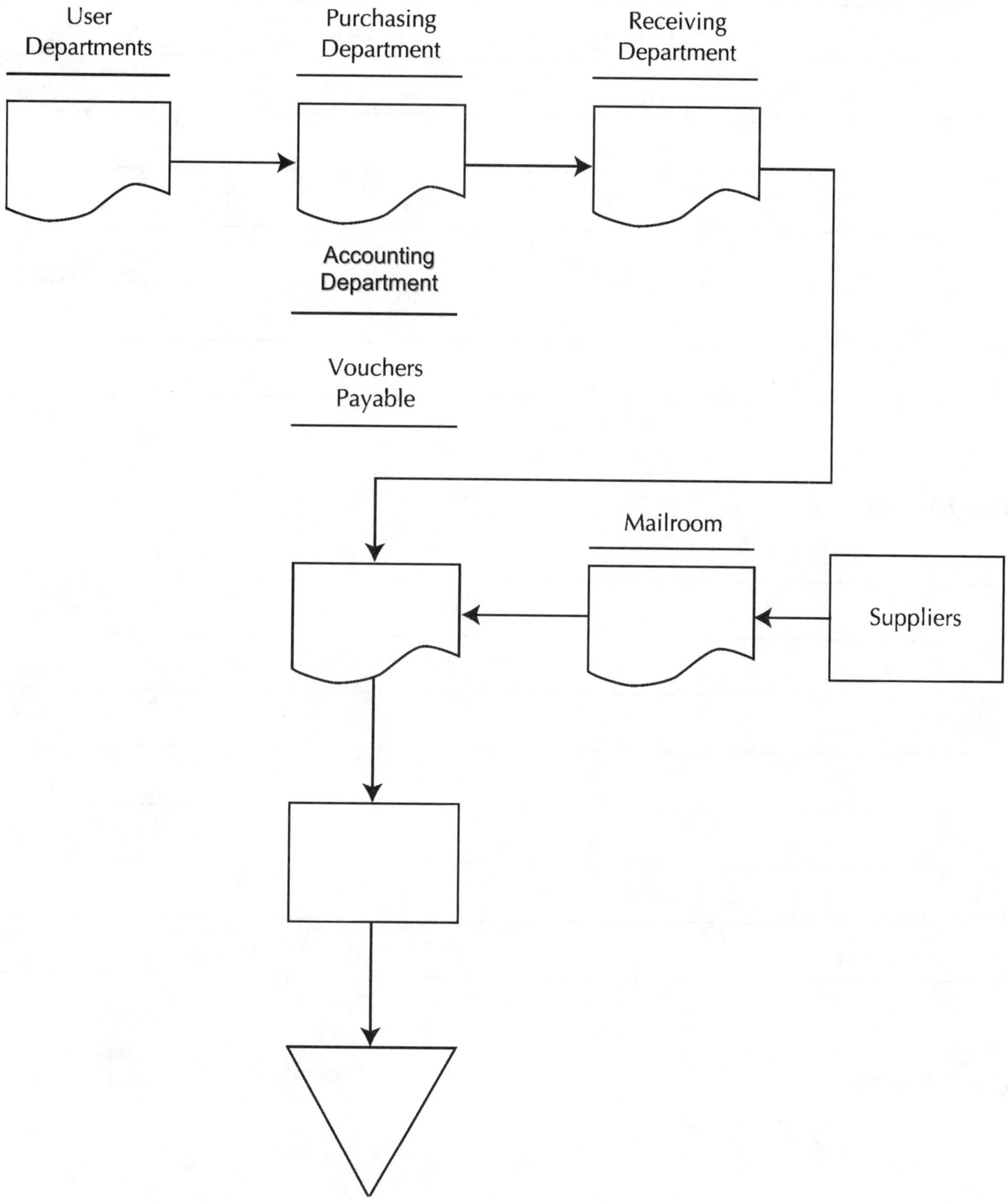

Problem 7Apx-4A

1. ____

2. ____

3. ____

4. ____

Exercise 7Apx-1B

1. ____

2. ____

3. ____

4. ____

Exercise 7Apx-2B

1. _____

2. _____

3. _____

4. _____

Name ______________________________

Exercise 7Apx-3B

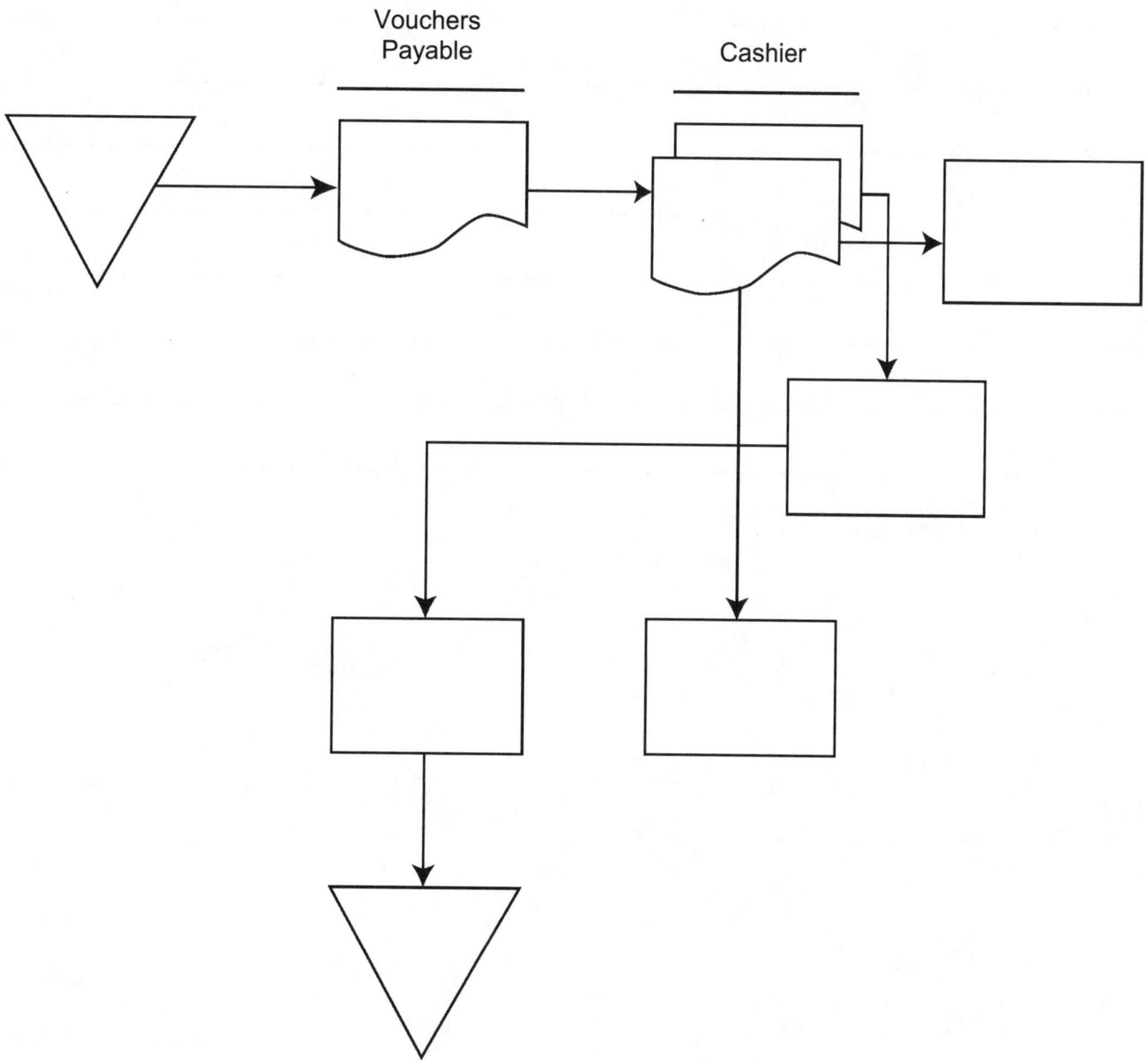

Problem 7Apx-4B

1. ______________________________

____

2. ______________________________

____

3. ______________________________

____

4. ______________________________

____

Name ______________________________

Exercise 8-1A

a. __________ regular hours × $10 per hour __________

b. __________ overtime hours × $15 per hour __________

c. Total gross wages __________

d. Federal income tax withholding (from tax tables in Figure 8-4) __________

e. Social Security withholding at 6.2% __________

f. Medicare withholding at 1.45% __________

g. Total withholding __________

h. Net pay __________

Exercise 8-2A

Exercise 8-3A

Exercise 8-4A

	Marital Status	Total Weekly Earnings	Number of Allowances	Amount of Withholding
a.	S	$347.60	2	
b.	S	451.50	1	
c.	M	481.15	3	
d.	S	490.52	0	
e.	M	701.89	5	

Exercise 8-5A

Cumul. Pay Before Current Weekly Payroll	Current Gross Pay	Year-to-Date Earnings	Soc. Sec. Maximum	Amount Over Max. Soc. Sec.	Amount Subject to Soc. Sec.	Soc. Sec. Tax Withheld	Medicare Tax Withheld
$ 22,000	$1,700		$110,100				
54,000	4,200		110,100				
107,500	3,925		110,100				
109,500	4,600		110,100				

Exercise 8-6A

GENERAL JOURNAL PAGE

	DATE	DESCRIPTION	POST. REF.	DEBIT	CREDIT	
1						1
2						2
3						3
4						4
5						5
6						6
7						7
8						8
9						9

Exercise 8-7A

GENERAL JOURNAL PAGE

	DATE	DESCRIPTION	POST. REF.	DEBIT	CREDIT	
1						1
2						2
3						3
4						4
5						5
6						6
7						7
8						8
9						9

Name ______________________

Problem 8-8A

1.

2.

GENERAL JOURNAL

PAGE

	DATE		DESCRIPTION	POST. REF.	DEBIT	CREDIT	
1							1
2							2
3							3
4							4
5							5
6							6
7							7
8							8
9							9
10							10
11							11
12							12
13							13
14							14
15							15

Problem 8-9A

1.

PAYROLL REGISTER

	NAME	NO. ALLOW.	MARIT. STATUS	EARNINGS				TAXABLE EARNINGS	
				REGULAR	OVERTIME	TOTAL	CUMULATIVE TOTAL	UNEMPLOY. COMP.	SOCIAL SECURITY
1									
2									
3									
4									
5									
6									
7									
8									
9									
10									
11									
12									
13									
14									

Problem 8-9A (Concluded)

FOR PERIOD ENDED 20--

DEDUCTIONS										
FEDERAL INCOME TAX	SOCIAL SECURITY TAX	MEDICARE TAX	CITY TAX	HEALTH INSUR.	OTHER		TOTAL	NET PAY	CK. NO.	
										1
										2
										3
										4
										5
										6
										7
										8
										9
										10
										11
										12
										13
										14

2.

GENERAL JOURNAL

PAGE

	DATE	DESCRIPTION	POST. REF.	DEBIT	CREDIT	
1						1
2						2
3						3
4						4
5						5
6						6
7						7
8						8
9						9
10						10
11						11
12						12
13						13
14						14

Problem 8-10A

EMPLOYEE EARNINGS RECORD

20 -- PERIOD ENDED	EARNINGS				TAXABLE EARNINGS		DEDUCTIONS	
	REGULAR	OVERTIME	TOTAL	CUMULATIVE TOTAL	UNEMPLOY. COMP.	SOCIAL SECURITY	FEDERAL INCOME TAX	SOCIAL SECURITY TAX

GENDER		DEPARTMENT	OCCUPATION	SOCIAL SECURITY NO.	MARITAL STATUS	ALLOW-ANCES
M	F					

Name ______________________________

Problem 8-10A (Concluded)

FOR PERIOD ENDED 20--

DEDUCTIONS						
MEDICARE TAX	CITY TAX	HEALTH INSURANCE	OTHER	TOTAL	CK. NO.	AMOUNT

PAY RATE	DATE OF BIRTH	DATE HIRED	NAME/ADDRESS	EMP. NO.

Exercise 8-1B

a. __________ regular hours × $12 per hour __________

b. __________ overtime hours × $18 per hour __________

c. Total gross wages __________

d. Federal income tax withholding (from tax tables in Figure 8-4) __________

e. Social Security withholding at 6.2% __________

f. Medicare withholding at 1.45% __________

g. Total withholding __________

h. Net pay __________

Exercise 8-2B

Exercise 8-3B

Exercise 8-4B

	Marital Status	Total Weekly Earnings	Number of Allowances	Amount of Withholding
a.	M	$546.00	4	
b.	M	390.00	3	
c.	S	461.39	2	
d.	M	522.88	2	
e.	S	612.00	0	

Exercise 8-5B

Cumul. Pay Before Current Weekly Payroll	Current Gross Pay	Year-to-Date Earnings	Soc. Sec. Maximum	Amount Over Max. Soc. Sec.	Amount Subject to Soc. Sec.	Soc. Sec. Tax Withheld	Medicare Tax Withheld
$ 31,000	$1,500		$110,100				
53,000	2,860		110,100				
107,200	3,140		110,100				
109,500	2,920		110,100				

Exercise 8-6B

GENERAL JOURNAL PAGE

	DATE	DESCRIPTION	POST. REF.	DEBIT	CREDIT	
1						1
2						2
3						3
4						4
5						5
6						6
7						7
8						8
9						9
10						10
11						11
12						12
13						13
14						14
15						15
16						16
17						17
18						18
19						19
20						20
21						21
22						22

Exercise 8-7B

GENERAL JOURNAL PAGE

	DATE		DESCRIPTION	POST. REF.	DEBIT	CREDIT	
1							1
2							2
3							3
4							4
5							5
6							6
7							7
8							8
9							9
10							10
11							11
12							12
13							13

Problem 8-8B

1.

Name ______________________________

Problem 8-8B (Concluded)

2.

GENERAL JOURNAL

PAGE

DATE		DESCRIPTION	POST. REF.	DEBIT	CREDIT

Problem 8-9B

1.

PAYROLL REGISTER

				EARNINGS				TAXABLE EARNINGS	
	NAME	NO. ALLOW.	MARIT. STATUS	REGULAR	OVERTIME	TOTAL	CUMULATIVE TOTAL	UNEMPLOY. COMP.	SOCIAL SECURITY
1									
2									
3									
4									
5									
6									
7									
8									
9									
10									
11									
12									
13									
14									

Name ______________________________

Problem 8-9B (Concluded)

FOR PERIOD ENDED 20--

DEDUCTIONS									
FEDERAL INCOME TAX	SOCIAL SECURITY TAX	MEDICARE TAX	CITY TAX	HEALTH INSUR.	OTHER	TOTAL	NET PAY	CK. NO.	
									1
									2
									3
									4
									5
									6
									7
									8
									9
									10
									11
									12
									13
									14

2.

GENERAL JOURNAL

PAGE

	DATE	DESCRIPTION	POST. REF.	DEBIT	CREDIT	
1						1
2						2
3						3
4						4
5						5
6						6
7						7
8						8
9						9
10						10
11						11
12						12
13						13
14						14

Problem 8-10B

EMPLOYEE EARNINGS RECORD

20 -- PERIOD ENDED	EARNINGS: REGULAR	EARNINGS: OVERTIME	EARNINGS: TOTAL	EARNINGS: CUMULATIVE TOTAL	TAXABLE EARNINGS: UNEMPLOY. COMP.	TAXABLE EARNINGS: SOCIAL SECURITY	DEDUCTIONS: FEDERAL INCOME TAX	DEDUCTIONS: SOCIAL SECURITY TAX

GENDER		DEPARTMENT	OCCUPATION	SOCIAL SECURITY NO.	MARITAL STATUS	ALLOW-ANCES
M	F					

Name ______________________________

Problem 8-10B (Concluded)

FOR PERIOD ENDED 20--

DEDUCTIONS						
MEDICARE TAX	CITY TAX	HEALTH INSURANCE	OTHER	TOTAL	CK. NO.	AMOUNT

PAY RATE	DATE OF BIRTH	DATE HIRED	NAME/ADDRESS	EMP. NO.

Mastery Problem

1.

PAYROLL REGISTER

				EARNINGS				TAXABLE EARNINGS	
	NAME	NO. ALLOW.	MARIT. STATUS	REGULAR	OVERTIME	TOTAL	CUMULATIVE TOTAL	UNEMPLOY. COMP.	SOCIAL SECURITY
1									
2									
3									
4									
5									
6									
7									
8									
9									
10									
11									
12									
13									
14									

3.

EMPLOYEE EARNINGS RECORD

	EARNINGS				TAXABLE EARNINGS		
20 -- PERIOD ENDED	REGULAR	OVERTIME	TOTAL	CUMULATIVE TOTAL	UNEMPLOY. COMP.	SOCIAL SECURITY	FEDERAL INCOME TAX
11/4	330 00	33 00	363 00	6,145 50	363 00	363 00	6 00
11/11	440 00	49 50	489 50	6,635 00	489 50	489 50	18 00
11/18							
11/25							

GENDER		DEPARTMENT	OCCUPATION	SOCIAL SECURITY NO.	MARITAL STATUS
M	F				

Mastery Problem (Continued)

FOR PERIOD ENDED 20--

DEDUCTIONS								
FEDERAL INCOME TAX	SOCIAL SECURITY TAX	MEDICARE TAX	STATE INCOME TAX	HEALTH INSURANCE	CREDIT UNION	TOTAL	NET PAY	CK. NO.
								1
								2
								3
								4
								5
								6
								7
								8
								9
								10
								11
								12
								13
								14

FOR PERIOD ENDED 20--

DEDUCTIONS						NET PAY	
SOCIAL SECURITY TAX	MEDICARE TAX	STATE INCOME TAX	HEALTH INSURANCE	CREDIT UNION	TOTAL	CK. NO.	AMOUNT
22 51	5 26	12 71		72 60	119 08	121	243 92
30 35	7 10	17 13		97 90	170 48	229	319 02

ALLOWANCES	PAY RATE	DATE OF BIRTH	DATE HIRED	NAME/ADDRESS	EMP. NO.

Mastery Problem (Concluded)

2.

GENERAL JOURNAL

PAGE

DATE		DESCRIPTION	POST. REF.	DEBIT	CREDIT

Name ______________________________

Challenge Problem

1.

GENERAL JOURNAL PAGE

	DATE		DESCRIPTION	POST. REF.	DEBIT	CREDIT	
1							1
2							2
3							3
4							4
5							5
6							6
7							7
8							8
9							9
10							10

2.

Exercise 9-1A

GENERAL JOURNAL PAGE

	DATE		DESCRIPTION	POST. REF.	DEBIT	CREDIT	
1							1
2							2
3							3
4							4
5							5
6							6
7							7

Exercise 9-2A

GENERAL JOURNAL PAGE

	DATE		DESCRIPTION	POST. REF.	DEBIT	CREDIT	
1							1
2							2
3							3
4							4
5							5
6							6
7							7

Exercise 9-3A

		Taxable Earnings	
Name	**Current Earnings**	**Unemploy. Comp.**	**Social Security**
Jordahl			
Keesling			
Palmer			
Soltis			
Stout			
Xia			
Total			

GENERAL JOURNAL PAGE

	DATE		DESCRIPTION	POST. REF.	DEBIT	CREDIT	
1							1
2							2
3							3
4							4
5							5
6							6
7							7

Exercise 9-4A

Exercise 9-5A

GENERAL JOURNAL

PAGE

	DATE		DESCRIPTION	POST. REF.	DEBIT	CREDIT	
1							1
2							2
3							3
4							4
5							5
6							6
7							7
8							8
9							9
10							10
11							11
12							12

Exercise 9-6A

1.

GENERAL JOURNAL

PAGE

	DATE		DESCRIPTION	POST. REF.	DEBIT	CREDIT	
1							1
2							2
3							3
4							4
5							5

2.

GENERAL JOURNAL

PAGE

	DATE		DESCRIPTION	POST. REF.	DEBIT	CREDIT	
1							1
2							2
3							3
4							4

Problem 9-7A

1.

Name	Current Earnings	Taxable Earnings: Unemploy. Comp.	Taxable Earnings: Social Security
Click, Katelyn			
Coombs, Michelle			
Faus, Erin			
Lenihan, Marcus			
McMahon, Drew			
Newell, Marg			
Stevens, Matt			
Total			

2.

GENERAL JOURNAL

PAGE

	DATE		DESCRIPTION	POST. REF.	DEBIT	CREDIT	
1							1
2							2
3							3
4							4
5							5
6							6
7							7
8							8
9							9
10							10

Name ______________________________

Problem 9-8A

1.

GENERAL JOURNAL

PAGE

DATE		DESCRIPTION	POST. REF.	DEBIT	CREDIT

Problem 9-8A (Continued)

GENERAL JOURNAL

PAGE

	DATE		DESCRIPTION	POST. REF.	DEBIT	CREDIT	
1							1
2							2
3							3
4							4
5							5
6							6
7							7
8							8
9							9
10							10
11							11
12							12
13							13
14							14
15							15
16							16
17							17
18							18
19							19
20							20
21							21
22							22
23							23
24							24
25							25
26							26
27							27
28							28
29							29
30							30
31							31
32							32
33							33
34							34
35							35

Problem 9-8A (Concluded)

2.

Cash 101

Employee Federal Income Tax Payable 211

Social Security Tax Payable 212

Medicare Tax Payable 213

Savings Bond Deductions Payable 218

FUTA Tax Payable 221

SUTA Tax Payable 222

Wages and Salaries Expense 511

Payroll Taxes Expense 530

Problem 9-9A

1.

GENERAL JOURNAL

PAGE

	DATE		DESCRIPTION	POST. REF.	DEBIT	CREDIT	
1							1
2							2
3							3
4							4
5							5
6							6

2.

GENERAL JOURNAL

PAGE

	DATE		DESCRIPTION	POST. REF.	DEBIT	CREDIT	
1							1
2							2
3							3
4							4
5							5
6							6

Name ______________________

Problem 9-9A (Concluded)

3.

GENERAL JOURNAL

PAGE

	DATE		DESCRIPTION	POST. REF.	DEBIT	CREDIT	
1							1
2							2
3							3
4							4
5							5

Exercise 9-1B

GENERAL JOURNAL

PAGE

	DATE		DESCRIPTION	POST. REF.	DEBIT	CREDIT	
1							1
2							2
3							3
4							4
5							5
6							6
7							7
8							8
9							9

Exercise 9-2B

GENERAL JOURNAL

PAGE

	DATE		DESCRIPTION	POST. REF.	DEBIT	CREDIT	
1							1
2							2
3							3
4							4
5							5
6							6
7							7
8							8

Exercise 9-3B

		Taxable Earnings	
Name	**Current Earnings**	**Unemploy. Comp.**	**Social Security**
Carlson			
Delgado			
Lewis			
Nixon			
Shippe			
Watts			
Total			

Name ______________________________

Exercise 9-3B (Concluded)

____

____

____

____

____

GENERAL JOURNAL PAGE

	DATE		DESCRIPTION	POST. REF.	DEBIT	CREDIT	
1							1
2							2
3							3
4							4
5							5
6							6
7							7

Exercise 9-4B: See page WP-302.

Exercise 9-5B

GENERAL JOURNAL PAGE

	DATE		DESCRIPTION	POST. REF.	DEBIT	CREDIT	
1							1
2							2
3							3
4							4
5							5
6							6
7							7
8							8
9							9
10							10
11							11
12							12
13							13
14							14

Exercise 9-4B

Exercise 9-6B

1.

GENERAL JOURNAL PAGE

	DATE		DESCRIPTION	POST. REF.	DEBIT	CREDIT	
1							1
2							2
3							3
4							4
5							5

2.

GENERAL JOURNAL PAGE

	DATE		DESCRIPTION	POST. REF.	DEBIT	CREDIT	
1							1
2							2
3							3
4							4
5							5

Name ______________________

Problem 9-7B

1.

		Taxable Earnings	
Name	**Current Earnings**	**Unemploy. Comp.**	**Social Security**
Ackers, Alice			
Conley, Dorothy			
Davis, James			
Lawrence, Kevin			
Rawlings, Judy			
Tanaka, Sumio			
Vadillo, Raynette			
Total			

2.

GENERAL JOURNAL

PAGE

	DATE		DESCRIPTION	POST. REF.	DEBIT	CREDIT	
1							1
2							2
3							3
4							4
5							5
6							6
7							7
8							8
9							9
10							10
11							11
12							12

Problem 9-8B

1.

GENERAL JOURNAL

PAGE

	DATE	DESCRIPTION	POST. REF.	DEBIT	CREDIT	
1						1
2						2
3						3
4						4
5						5
6						6
7						7
8						8
9						9
10						10
11						11
12						12
13						13
14						14
15						15
16						16
17						17
18						18
19						19
20						20
21						21
22						22
23						23
24						24
25						25
26						26
27						27
28						28
29						29
30						30
31						31
32						32
33						33
34						34
35						35
36						36

Name ______________________________

Problem 9-8B (Continued)

GENERAL JOURNAL

PAGE

	DATE		DESCRIPTION	POST. REF.	DEBIT	CREDIT	
1							1
2							2
3							3
4							4
5							5
6							6
7							7
8							8
9							9
10							10
11							11
12							12
13							13
14							14
15							15
16							16
17							17
18							18
19							19
20							20
21							21
22							22
23							23
24							24
25							25
26							26
27							27
28							28
29							29
30							30
31							31
32							32
33							33
34							34
35							35

Problem 9-8B (Concluded)

2.

Cash 101

Employee Federal Income Tax Payable 211

Social Security Tax Payable 212

Medicare Tax Payable 213

Savings Bond Deductions Payable 218

FUTA Tax Payable 221

SUTA Tax Payable 222

Wages and Salaries Expense 511

Payroll Taxes Expense 530

Problem 9-9B

1.

GENERAL JOURNAL PAGE

	DATE		DESCRIPTION	POST. REF.	DEBIT	CREDIT	
1							1
2							2
3							3
4							4
5							5
6							6

2.

GENERAL JOURNAL PAGE

	DATE		DESCRIPTION	POST. REF.	DEBIT	CREDIT	
1							1
2							2
3							3
4							4
5							5
6							6

Problem 9-9B (Concluded)

3.

GENERAL JOURNAL

PAGE

	DATE		DESCRIPTION	POST. REF.	DEBIT	CREDIT	
1							1
2							2
3							3
4							4

Mastery Problem

1., 2., and 3.

GENERAL JOURNAL

PAGE

	DATE		DESCRIPTION	POST. REF.	DEBIT	CREDIT	
1							1
2							2
3							3
4							4
5							5
6							6
7							7
8							8
9							9
10							10
11							11
12							12
13							13
14							14
15							15
16							16
17							17
18							18
19							19
20							20
21							21
22							22
23							23
24							24
25							25
26							26
27							27
28							28
29							29
30							30
31							31
32							32
33							33
34							34
35							35

Mastery Problem (Concluded)

GENERAL JOURNAL

PAGE

	DATE		DESCRIPTION	POST. REF.	DEBIT	CREDIT	
1							1
2							2
3							3
4							4
5							5
6							6
7							7
8							8
9							9
10							10
11							11
12							12
13							13
14							14
15							15
16							16
17							17
18							18
19							19
20							20
21							21
22							22
23							23
24							24
25							25
26							26
27							27
28							28
29							29
30							30
31							31
32							32
33							33
34							34
35							35

Challenge Problem

1.

2.

GENERAL JOURNAL PAGE

	DATE		DESCRIPTION	POST. REF.	DEBIT	CREDIT	
1							1
2							2
3							3
4							4
5							5
6							6
7							7

3.